Visions, Visitations
& THE
Voice of God

Prophetic Activations to develop your ability to see and hear in the Spirit.

Visions, Visitations
& THE
# Voice of God

Lyn Packer

Originally published by XP Publishing
A department of XP Ministries
P.O. Box 1017, Maricopa, Arizona 85139

ISBN-13: 978-1-936101-29-0

ISBN-10: 1-936101-29-7

Dedication

This book is dedicated to my husband Rob,
who has been my greatest supporter. He has believed in me
since the beginning, seeing the potential no one else saw.
I love you.

Also to my kids,
Dan & Aimee, Tanya & Phil,
who are such an encouragement to me in everything I do.

Thanks to all the friends who helped me "test drive" the
activations.
I so appreciate you all.

Carol & Michelle,
thanks for your work in whipping this book into shape.

And to Patricia,

your encouragement means so much.

Endorsements

"The activations truly lead you on a journey, which is a discovery of self and of the depths of God's heart for you. Each one inevitably draws you in closer to Jesus and leaves you with a greater sense of being known and a stronger desire to make Him known. As I did them, they brought to mind Psalm 26:2 - Test me O Lord, and know my heart, then lead me on in the way everlasting."

- Erin Bradley

"These activations have been such a blessing and a valuable tool in training me to sharpen my ability to see and hear what the Lord is speaking to me. I'd thoroughly recommend this book to anyone wanting to go deeper in his or her relationship with the Lord and develop their spiritual senses."

- Rochelle Woods

"2 Corinthians speaks of casting down imaginations and anything that exalts itself above God. I have learned through the teaching and activations in this book that our minds and imaginations were designed by God and for God."

- Dennis Shipman

"The activations have encouraged me to look closer at what God is showing me and ask Him questions. As I press in, He takes me deeper and gives me more revelation. He has shown me more about what He thinks of me and other people. It's amazing how much more clarity God gives us when we ask for it."

-Denise Marsden

"Lyn teaches and ministers, passionately and prophetically, combining heart and mind in a way that reveals and applies revelational truth, resulting in encounters with God that change lives. Rob & Lyn have a capacity, in a corporate setting, to break through to new horizons in the Spirit and take folk with them."

- Pastor Kevin Hight,
Avalon Baptist Church, Wellington, NZ

"Lyn's prophetic anointing is displayed in a powerful yet gentle way. She and her husband, Rob Packer, carry powerful gifts that change the spiritual climate of the places God calls them to minister. You will be blessed, encouraged and challenged through their ministry."

-Pastor Vicki Strickland,
Lead Pastor, Blueridge Christian Center, Arizona, USA
Founder Global Outreach Ministries

"Lyn has a prophetic edge that is inspiring. She and her husband are a pastor's true friend. Each time they come they leave a beautiful deposit of the Spirit. They carry a true prophetic voice through our nation."

- Pastor Ray Watson,
Pursuit Church, Auckland, NZ

Contents

Foreword

by Patricia King

God is truly pouring out His Spirit upon all flesh in these last days and many believers are experiencing a variety of legitimate divine encounters. There is indeed an acceleration of visitation, miracles, signs, and wonders in this hour. As a result, it is vital that we discern the true from the false. It is equally important that we understand how to fully embrace the encounters the Lord grants us and grow in prophetic seasoning and maturity through the process.

Lyn Packer, in her book *Visions, Visitations and The Voice of God*, lovingly invites the reader to engage in a deep personal relationship with Holy Spirit and to enthusiastically embrace God-given encounters. She teaches how to clearly identify and discern God's voice and gives understanding on how to interpret and activate Spirit-inspired revelation.

Through the use of scriptures, in addition to testimonies of her own personal spiritual journey, Lyn builds confidence in the reader as she invites them to experience all God offers. As you read this book, you will be excited to discover that there is an effectual door leading into God-given encounter with your name on it! Jesus secured it for you through His finished work on the cross two thousand years ago.

I was particularly impressed with the activation section of this book as I am convinced that the exercises of faith application will help the reader to unlock, identify and validate the reality of their spiritual potential and Kingdom encounters.

Enjoy discovery!

Patricia King
XPmedia, Founder and President

Introduction

The Church is undergoing a radical transformation and reformation. There is a growing hunger for supernatural encounters with God and for more of the supernatural power of God to be released. We are in a season where revelatory experiences are increasing in frequency. More and more people are experiencing and talking about their encounters with the Lord.

Until recently, if a Christian had a vision, a supernatural encounter or an experience from God, they might not have shared their experience for fear of not being believed or understood. The Bible is filled with testimonies of people who had supernatural visions and encounters with God both in the earthly and heavenly realms. These experiences with God did not stop when the New Testament was completed. Valid experiences with God have carried on throughout church history and are increasing in these days.

God is doing amazing things in the world! We need to understand what the Word of God says about what is happening today, so we can know how to co-operate with Him and not be deceived.

In the past, the Church has been very fearful about being deceived in relation to experiencing the supernatural realms. Because of what we have seen in the occult and in the New Age movement, we have wrongly assumed that supernatural occurrences originate with the devil. It is important to understand that revelation, truth, and the supernatural realm originated with God and not the devil. Satan is not a creator. He counterfeits what is true in order to bring many into bondage through his deceptive ways.

We have often reacted with unhealthy extremes because of failing to understand all that God made available to us. We often labelled as "deception" things that were true. We have sometimes had more faith in the devil's ability to deceive than in God's ability to keep us in the truth.

Some experiences that Holy Spirit will lead us into may feel unfamiliar and out of our comfort zone. This may mean that we need to work through an initial phase of awkwardness as we get used to the different ways that God reveals Himself to us. We can however, definitely expect to hear and recognize His voice more clearly over time.

Because many things we experience are often subjective, it is wise to have some guidelines that will help us understand and negotiate those experiences. Hence, this book and others like it are being released to give good foundations to build on. Close study of Scripture is also very essential for correct interpretation of what we experience.

Experiencing God

We are sometimes taught that we should not be experience oriented. But the truth is we cannot be alive without experience. Every single thing we do in life is an experience, whether combing our hair, reading a book, or praying. To live is to experience.

It cannot be otherwise. Even when we pass from this life, we continue to experience the reality of the Kingdom of God for all eternity.

Why is it said, "Don't seek experience" when it comes to relationship with God? Many have bought into a lie perpetuated by the enemy that intends to dumb down its prey until their relationship with God is nothing more than reading a historic book. You cannot have relationship without experience. It is impossible. Although we are not to worship experience itself, it is only by experience we come to learn and know the one we are in relationship with. We know each other by experiencing things together - good and bad; by talking, observing and sharing our hearts with each other.

In his book, *The Supernatural Power of a Transformed Mind*, Bill Johnson says:

> "Understanding is an experience – we must require an experience of what we believe... In our culture we define understanding as nothing more than cognitive reasoning... but in Eastern culture, which is the culture of Scripture, understanding is an experience. It means engaging our five senses. In Matt. 13:19, in the parable of the sower and the seeds, the Greek word for understanding means– 'learning which takes place through the five senses.' Biblical learning (revelation) takes place in the spirit first, and as we obey the Spirit of God, our spirit communicates it to our minds so that we can intellectually understand."

For the last few centuries many western Christians lived their Christianity from a Greek mindset and point of view, instead of the Hebrew mindset that influenced the early Church. The Greek mindset infers, "You know something when you understand it as a concept." The Hebrew mindset embraces the belief, "You don't truly know something until you experience and understand it." God is bringing about a transformation of our minds in this hour, leading to the emergence of a truly supernatural Church rightly displaying who God is, because they have *experienced* who He is.

How wonderful it is when we, like Moses, daily encounter God as He speaks to us "face to face as a friend" (*Ex. 33:11*). This is how we are changed more into His likeness, from one degree of glory to another (*2 Cor. 3:18*).

For Further Study

The Supernatural Power of a Transformed Mind - Bill Johnson

1

Living from Two Realms

ot every Christian understands how to hear God or how to see into the heavenly realms. Yet, the ability to see and hear what the Lord is doing is something that is absolutely essential and foundational to the Christian walk. Paul tells us in 2 Cor. 4:18 to "fix our eyes not on what is seen, but on what is unseen, for what is seen is temporary and what is unseen is eternal."

The seen realm mentioned in this verse refers to everything in our physical earthly and temporal plane. Everything outside of that is considered the unseen. We experience the seen realm with our five senses and we experience the unseen through our spiritual senses. We will look more at that in the next chapter. The eternal, unseen realm is the realm where God dwells. This heavenly realm is actually more real than the temporal realm that we live in. One day, all that we can see in this present earthly realm will be gone, but the eternal realm is forever.

We are told by Paul to fix our eyes not on what is seen, but on what is unseen. Fixed eyes are eyes that are focused, both with the intent to see and the ability to see. Paul doesn't present it as an optional extra. He emphatically tells us what we should be doing and how we should be seeing. Paul teaches that we must live in two realms: the seen and the unseen, the eternal and the temporal. The eternal is to be the predominant realm we live in. How do we see what is unseen? We see with the eyes of our spirit.

In John 5:19, Jesus teaches that seeing and hearing what God is doing was vital to how He lived and ministered. I believe He experienced revelatory encounters with God daily. He also wants us to experience God in that same way. Jesus lived two realms simultaneously, with the emphasis being on the eternal, affecting and changing the temporal. He alluded to this when He said to Nicodemus, "No one has ascended into heaven, but He who descended from heaven: the Son of Man who is in heaven." (John 3:13 KJV)

Jesus knew that true relationship and the life of the Spirit could not just be based on what was written in a book. The Pharisees had the Word of God, yet they lived a life that was lacking in relationship with God and His power. By His lifestyle, Jesus showed us that true Christian life is lived best when we are able to see what the Father is doing and hear what He is saying. Jesus knew how to access the heavenly realms and He lived from that perspective. Jesus showed us what it is all about: Relationship! It's about experiencing God in our daily life and co-operating with Him in what He shows us. In fact, we can't legally access revelation from the spirit realm without going through Jesus. He is the door (John 10:7).

Revelation -
A Call to Intimacy and Co-Operation

This book teaches a simple foundation of understanding needed to wisely use the activations it contains. This book is all about intimacy, revelation and co-operation with God. Each of the activations in this book will help take you into an experience with God. Experience, from God's perspective, is always an invitation to intimacy, revelation and co-operation. In fact, God will often deliberately hide deep revelation inside experience because He wants us to pursue Him.

Our primary call, regardless of our gift, is intimacy with God. To know Him and be known by Him is foundational, and from that place your gift flows, releasing the heart of God to others. It is never just about the gift.

Your intimacy with God is already established through Christ's finished work on the cross. If you have accepted Christ, you are now forever in a place of intimacy with God through Him. In fact, you cannot be any closer to God than you already are. You are in Christ and Christ is in you. Through Christ, you are positioned in a state of intimacy with the God who created everything!

If we are as intimate with God as we can be, does that mean we don't need to know or experience more of Him than we do right now? There is always more of the Lord for us to know and experience, but that's different from our state of intimacy. We will forever discover more of the wonder of who He is. We can and should desire to encounter deeper friendship with Him. No matter how many millions of years we exist, we will never plumb the depths of who God is! The finite will never be able to exhaust or fully understand the infinite. Our desire should be to know God more and more, each passing day.

Activating Prayer

Father, I thank You for the Spirit of Wisdom and Revelation. Thank You for desiring to give me revelation as an invitation to intimacy and co-operation with You. I long for all of You! Therefore, I ask that You would grant me the spirit of wisdom and revelation to operate at a deeper level in my life. Draw me into deeper intimacy and co-operation with You. I receive that now by faith. I look forward with expectation to walking a life of revelation, bringing me into the depths of You, deeper than I have ever known. Thank you for that, Lord.

2

The Prophetic Senses

You are a three part being: spirit, soul and body. You are one person, with three interwoven parts, functioning together to make a whole. Your spirit primarily helps you relate to the spirit realm. Your soul relates to the relational realm and your body relates to the physical realm. Body, soul and spirit can also overlap in their functions.

Your natural man has five physical senses: sight, hearing, taste, smell and touch. Your spirit has those same senses as well as the sense of discernment (perception). You have a natural sense of discernment but also the spiritual sense, which is called the "gift of discernment."

Natural discernment helps you relate to the natural realm (emotional and relational), while the gift of discernment helps you discern in the supernatural realm. You are able to discern between the four different types of spirits that may be at work in any situation: 1) the Holy Spirit 2) the human spirit 3) heavenly spirits 4) demonic spirits. [1]

To understand and walk in the spiritual life God has for us, we need to be able to recognize and interpret those things we see, smell, feel, hear, taste and discern in the Spirit. We must learn to use all these senses to receive revelation. The following are some examples of discerning, using the different senses.

- I was in a meeting one night when, suddenly, the fragrance of fresh baked bread filled the room. The smell was so strong! I could smell it with my physical senses and yet, it was a spiritually generated fragrance. Others also smelled it. One man even went outside to check if there was a bakery nearby. There wasn't - the aroma was only in the auditorium. That smell of fresh bread was a fragrance from heaven, telling us there was fresh revelation for us that night (*Matt. 4:4*). This spiritual fragrance was so real that I was unsure whether I initially discerned it using the spiritual sense of smell, the physical sense of smell, or both.

- While I was attending my first Glory School, taught by Patricia King in Tucson, Arizona, I discerned that an angel was standing next to me at the end of our row. A few minutes later, I stood up and stepped into the aisle. Although I never saw anything with my physical eyes, the angel was there. This was confirmed when I walked into its very tangible presence and was knocked backward by the impact. My physical body and senses were influenced and impacted by the reality of the unseen.

- Many years ago, I was in a meeting where we were due to speak and I heard a rumbling sound. Initially,

22

I thought it was created by a lot of trucks going past the building but it continued to get louder and louder. Then suddenly, the whole front of the auditorium disappeared from my sight! I saw an open-eye vision into the spirit realm. There were many heavenly chariots, horses and angels forming into ranks. Row after row they stretched. The angel in the lead chariot got out and bowed. I asked the Lord, "What are they doing?" I felt Him say that they were awaiting His orders to be sent to do a particular work that He had for them. At that stage in my walk with the Lord, I didn't know to ask more questions in order to receive more revelation and soon the vision faded. I was unsure whether the hearing was physical or spiritual. Although it felt like I heard it with my natural ears, I discovered it was spiritual since no one else heard it.

These are just a few examples of different senses being used to see or discern spiritual realities. Often, revelation will be received through multiple senses simultaneously. Some people will find certain senses are better developed than others but they can all be developed with time and practice. We should seek to do so.

Our physical senses are not always a true indicator, or interpreter, of what is happening in the spirit realm. If we work solely from our natural senses, we may discern wrongly - with our soul, and not by the Spirit of God. We must learn to rightly assess what we see and hear with our natural senses.

In Philippians 3:10, the Apostle Paul speaks of his desire for a deeper relationship with Christ: "That I may know (*ginosko*) Him and the power of His resurrection and the fellowship of His sufferings, being conformed to His death…" Paul was not writing here about an "intellectual" knowing.

The *Tyndale Bible Dictionary* defines the Greek word *ginosko* as follows:

> The word "know" or "knowledge" occurs more than 1,600 times in the Bible. The specific connotation of the word group provides insight into the basic messages of both the OT and the NT. The Hebrew view of man is one of differentiated totality—the heart, soul, and mind are so interrelated that they cannot be separated. "To know" thus involves the whole being and is not simply an action of the mind. The heart is sometimes identified as the organ of knowledge (cf. Ps. 49:3; Is. 6:10). *The implication is that knowledge involves both will and emotions… "To know God" involves relationship, fellowship, concern, and experience.* [2]

In Hebrew, the word for "to know" is: *Yada*. *Yada* does not mean to know intellectually. *Yada* essentially means, "to discern, as through the five senses." This root word occurs over 900 times in scripture and expresses multitude shades of knowledge gained by the senses.

The Bible says that we have the "mind of Christ" (*1 Cor. 2:16*). To have the "mind of Christ" is not referring to intellectual understanding. It speaks of understanding that includes our mind, heart, imagination, will, emotions, and the ability to discern. Our relationship with Jesus Christ is not just a logical understanding. It is an intimate relationship in which we know Him with our mind, experience, and senses.

Activating Prayer

Lord, I surrender myself afresh to You today. I surrender my eyes. I surrender my ears. I surrender all my senses to You. Awaken and activate them to receive revelation. Through their correct use, draw me into a place of fresh revelation. Grant me the wisdom to know how to walk in the revelation You give me. I receive that awakening now by faith, in Jesus name. I expect to hear and see with fresh clarity from now on.

[1] *The School of the Seers* - Jonathan Welton
[2] *Tyndale Bible Dictionary* - Tyndale House Publishers, 2001
[3] *Theological Wordbook of the Old Testament* - Moody Press, 1

3

Speak to Me, Lord

Sometimes people tell me that they don't hear God speak to them. However, the issue is not *whether* we can hear God's voice (because scripture tells us that we can). The real issue is learning to *recognize* God's voice when He speaks to us.

Jesus teaches that His sheep hear and know His voice (*John 10:27*). If we are one of His sheep, a child of God, then we can know His voice when He speaks to us. God wants us to hear Him! When we hear His voice, it brings life and favor into our lives. In Proverbs 8:34 we read, "Blessed is the man who listens to me, watching daily at my doors...for whoever finds me finds life and receives favor from the Lord."

Throughout scripture, we see time and time again God speaking to His people. Sometimes it is stated clearly how He spoke to them, such as when Moses heard God speak from a burning bush (*Ex. 3:2*), or when God spoke to Mary through the angel, Gabriel (*Luke 1:26-35*). On another occasion, He spoke to Saul in the midst of a bright light (*Acts 9:3*). But there are many other times when it is not so clear how He spoke – whether it was in a vision, through internal, revelatory thoughts, or an audible voice.

Job 33:14 states that God speaks in different ways, but we don't always recognize His voice. Later, we will look at all the different ways we receive revelation. For now, I just want to address our ability to hear God through the most common ways we receive revelation. If we don't understand how we hear God in these ways, we will miss a lot of what He says to us.

The most common ways we receive revelation from God are:

1. Through the scriptures (Logos and Rhema words)
2. The still, small voice of God (God thoughts or visual impressions)
3. Teachings
4. Prophecy (The personal, quickened word from God for us.)

Through the Scriptures
(LOGOS AND RHEMA WORDS)

To explain quickly how we hear through the scriptures: *Logos* is the written Word of God, what we know as the scriptures. It is important to read the scripture as it reveals truth. *Rhema* is a Holy Spirit quickened word. A rhema word can be a quickening of a scripture verse as we read our bibles or a word direct from God through other means. When we are waiting on the Lord in prayer, He can speak to our heart and mind a rhema word. A "rhema word" is Spirit to spirit communication; the Spirit of God communicating with our spirit. It initially bypasses the mind, but the mind may come to understand it later as we process what God spoke.

The Still, Small Voice of God
(GOD THOUGHTS OR VISUAL IMPRESSIONS)

The most common way we receive revelation, apart from the "quickened" word in scripture is the still, small voice of God. This comes to us as God-inspired thoughts and visual impressions.

Some individuals have problems recognizing when God is speaking, because they assume all the thoughts they have originate from their mind. But that is not necessarily so. Some thoughts originate from the spirit realm. Both God and the demonic have the capacity to speak to us in that realm. We read in Scripture that there are "arguments" and "high things that exalt themself against the knowledge of God" and that we are to bring those thoughts into captivity to the obedience of Christ. (*2 Cor. 10:4-5*)

We need to understand the difference between thoughts of the *mind*, thoughts of the *heart*, and thoughts from the *spirit realm*. Thoughts of the human mind are usually analytical, whereas, thoughts of the heart or from the spirit realm are spontaneous. So, some of my thoughts are analytical, originating with me and some come spontaneously to me. Spontaneous thoughts usually originate from one of three places: my heart or spirit, the Holy Spirit living within me, or an evil spirit trying to put his thoughts and ideas on me.

Auditory Communication

The still, small voice of God is usually "heard" as a spontaneous flow of thoughts to our mind or pictures and impressions seen with the "the eyes of our heart."

In fact, one of the Hebrew words for prophecy is *nabi*, which means to "bubble up" spontaneously. In other words, the prophetic person hears the voice of God bubbling up as a spontaneous flow within his spirit and heart. Often, immediately after that spontaneous thought, our mind kicks into operation and tells us we are probably making it up and we can't really be hearing from God. At this point we have a choice to make: we have to decide whether we are going to listen to our mind, or believe we have heard from God.

Why does God speak in a still, small voice? One reason is that it sharpens our listening skills and causes us to draw closer to the Lord to hear Him. It brings us to a place of stillness, so we can listen for Him to speak, and it stretches and grows our faith.

How do we recognize God when He speaks? When God speaks, He will never contradict His Word, His heart for people, or His character. Spontaneous thoughts in our mind that line up with God's Word, heart and character can most often be recognized as thoughts from God and not our carnal flesh or the devil.

We can recognize thoughts from our carnal flesh because they are hostile to God (*Rom. 8:7*). We can also recognize thoughts from the devil, because anything he speaks is based on lies (*John 8:44*). His words have the goal of stealing from us, killing the life of the Spirit within us, and destroying us (*John 10:10*).

Visual Speech

The term "visual speech" may sound like a misnomer, but it isn't. Habakkuk refers to it in chapter two when he says, "...I will watch to see what He will say to me." We are so used to the term "hearing" applying to hearing with our ears, yet God often speaks through visions and dreams (*Job 33:14-16*).

29

There are many verses that refer to receiving visions of all sorts but in the book of Daniel, he shares about receiving visions in his mind or heart (*Dan. 4:5, 10, 13; 7:7*). In these scriptures, Daniel is speaking about visual impressions or inner visions.

Understanding How We See

Your internal vision center is one of your most important spiritual senses. The Bible calls this vision center the "eyes of your heart." It is involved in every vision, dream, and thought in both the natural and spiritual realm. Your vision center has many purposes. It helps you receive revelation and see into the spirit realm, as well as enabling you to be a dreamer and creator like God.

The phrases in scripture: *eyes of the heart, eyes of the mind* and *eyes of your understanding,* all refer to the same function: our ability to see vision internally, or receive revelation in our mind or heart. In the original languages of scripture, they all refer to faculties of the mind or imagination (see reference notes below).

Today in modern English, we don't usually use the term, "eyes of our heart." We call that vision center by another name: the imagination. Your imagination is where you receive and see internal vision. All internal, visual revelation sourced in God will come to the "eyes of your heart" (your imagination or vision center) from your spirit, so your mind can grasp and understand spirit-received revelation.

Over the centuries, we have misunderstood and therefore abused our imagination. We have often allowed it to be filled with all sorts of images that defile it so that it needs to be cleansed and sanctified in order to receive clear revelation from God.

In the book of Genesis, we see God's imagination and

thoughts manifested physically in the earthly realm as He spoke creation into existence. Mankind was made in His image and received that ability to imagine, conceive vision, and see it brought to manifested fruition. Mankind's mind and imagination were darkened and became "vain" as a result of the fall. From the fall until Jesus' death and resurrection, we see that man's imagination (eyes of his heart and mind) was recorded as being "vain," "darkened" (*Rom. 1:21*), or "evil" (*Gen. 6:5*).

Romans 1:21-22 tells us why this happened:

"Although they knew God, they glorified Him not as God, neither were thankful; but became vain in their imaginations, and their foolish heart was darkened." (KJV)

In Ephesians 1:18, Paul prayed that "the eyes of your heart (NASB)/understanding (KJV) would be enlightened." So, we know there is the capability for a renewed mind and imagination.

In the above verse, the word "understanding" comes from the Greek word *dianoia*, which means deep thought, imagination, mind, and understanding.

Paul instructs us to be transformed by the renewing of our mind (*Rom. 12:2*). In this verse, the renewing and transformation of our mind and its faculties is expected. It's not an optional extra.

The word "mind" in this verse, is the same Greek word used in Eph. 1:18: *dianoia*. So we see that our mind or imagination can be renewed and transformed.

Our imagination (eyes of our heart/mind) is neither good nor bad in itself. It is simply a function of how God made us. How we use it and to whom we surrender it, determines whether it will become darkened or enlightened. If we fill our imagination with violence and rubbish, it will become darkened. In this case, we have surrendered it (knowingly or unknowingly) to the devil. If we surrender it to the Holy Spirit and fill it with good things, it will become enlightened.

"Finally, brothers, whatever is true, whatever is noble, whatever is right, whatever is pure, whatever is lovely, whatever is admirable - if anything is excellent or praiseworthy - think about such things." (*Phil. 4:8 NIV*)

Weigh What You Hear

When it comes to hearing God, whether by speech or by vision, there are two extremes we need to avoid. The first is, mistaking the voice of God for our own thoughts or imagination. This causes us to dismiss the voice of God before we've considered what we've heard and weighed it properly. The other extreme is to think that everything that comes into our mind is from God. While I believe we do hear God a lot more than we give ourselves credit for, this extreme can result in deception and pride.

We need to carefully check out and weigh the words we believe God is speaking. I Thessalonians 5:19-21 says, "Do not quench the Spirit, do not despise prophecies but test everything and hold fast to what is good."

While we definitely believe that God speaks today through many different means, it is always wise to confirm what we hear. We need to weigh what we hear against these three things:

1. The Word of God – scripture
2. The heart of God for mankind
3. The character of God, or His values which His kingdom
   is built on.

True communication from God will not contradict those three things. Don't be afraid to invite mature Christians to offer their discernment and counsel. It is always wise to walk in accountability.

There may be periods of time that God is silent when you pray - you have positioned yourself to listen, yet hear nothing. This can be so frustrating and, if not careful, you will begin striving to hear. During those times of silence, it is wise to check if there is anything that God has already spoken to you that you've not responded to or put into practice. Often, our disobedience to do what He has already said can cause a block in hearing clearly.

Activating Prayer

Father, I repent for wrongly using the eyes of my heart. Forgive me for allowing my vision center and my imagination to be filled with rubbish and things that are contrary to Your Word, heart and character. Cleanse and sanctify the eyes of my heart, my imagination, so that I may more easily receive revelation from You. I ask that You open my physical eyes and the eyes of my heart to see beyond the natural, into the spiritual realms. I want to receive the revelations You long to give me. Anoint my eyes with salve (Rev. 3:18) so that I may see.

Take some time here, to confess anything specific the Lord convicts you of. Tell Him your desires, regarding your ability to see and hear Him.

For Further Study

How to Hear God's Voice - Mark Virkler
The School of the Seers - Jonathan Welton
Ecstatic Prophecy - Stacey Campbell
The Seer - James Goll

4

Faith or Sovereign Act of God

I have been a Christian for many years now. Until a few years ago, when I occasionally received visions or experiences like smelling heavenly fragrances and feeling the physical touch of angels or the Holy Spirit, I would hope that one-day, if it was God's will, I would have another. "After all," I thought, "visions and encounters are sovereign acts of God that He gives to whom He wills when He feels like it." I didn't realize that I was playing into the hands of the enemy with those thoughts. I didn't realize that subconsciously, there were some things I believed that were wrong. Things like:

- If you are "lucky" or "blessed" you will have experiences.

- People who have more experiences are more favored by God.

- People who have more experiences are more spiritual than I am.

- People who have more dramatic experiences, like open-eyed visions, are more spiritually mature than I am.

It sounds silly when you see it written out like that, doesn't it? But those were the unconscious, underlying beliefs that I had and I am not alone! Many Christians have those same underlying beliefs, concerning visions and spiritual experiences. Now obviously, God loves it when His kids press in to know Him and develop their relationship with Him, but does He love them more than others? Are spiritual experiences "rewards" for maturity?

I don't believe that God loves some people more than others or that He uses experiences as rewards for growth and maturity. Scripture does teach us, however, that He rewards those who diligently seek Him (*Heb. 11:6*). It does not say what that reward is, but I tend to think that the greater part of that reward is in knowing Him more. No matter how wonderful experiences are, they are simply a means the Lord uses to bless us and bring us closer to Him. They are not, and never were, intended to be the focus.

I used to believe that spiritual experiences, like visions, were sovereign acts of God. I thought I had to wait until God felt like giving me an experience before I would have one. But I have since discovered that experience with God and revelation can be accessed by faith, just as I access everything else in my Christian walk by faith. Of course, God still can and does give me revelation sovereignly. God is sovereign and can initiate anything at anytime He desires, but I no longer have to wait or depend on that as being my only hope to accessing revelation.

Jesus said, "Therefore I tell you, whatever you ask for in prayer, believe that you have received it and it will be yours" (*Mark 11:24 NIV*). He lived a revelatory life and taught us that we can access anything in His Kingdom, by faith.

Jonathan Welton says, "Faith should always lead us into an experience of what we are having faith for.... Faith is the key that unlocks the door to experience."

Bill Johnson says, "Any doctrine that does not require of it a corresponding experience is invalid." I wonder how much of what we know has been invalidated and just become head knowledge because we have not cemented it into our lives by experience? Living the Christian life by head knowledge alone is an invalid way to live it, according to Scripture.

Over the centuries, many truths in scripture have been received by faith, experienced, and are now lived out by thousands upon thousands. The forerunners accessed God's promises by faith. For example, the modern church lives out of Martin Luther's revelation regarding salvation by grace, through faith in Christ. As a result, anyone who desires to be saved is saved, through faith in Christ.

Today, many live in the experience of the baptism of the Holy Spirit because someone received the revelation, experienced it, and shared it. They pressed through in faith and broke it open for us to live in the experience of that revelation.

One day my husband, Rob, was having time with the Lord when he saw a vision of a door in a heavenly place. The door was to a treasury room that had our name on it. Upon trying the door, it appeared locked. Then a voice told him to push harder, that the door was not locked but was merely stiff through lack of use and unbelief. It was a gentle rebuke and encouragement from the Lord, reminding us to use our faith to access the resources we needed. Just knowing that provision was there for us, wasn't enough. Faith had to be used, along with constant access, to keep the door free. It is like this with all things in the walk of faith.

We can read a verse from scripture and give mental assent to its truth, but that promise doesn't get activated in our life unless faith is added to it. Hebrews 4:2 tells us that the gospel was preached to certain people but the word they heard didn't do them any good, because they didn't mix faith with it.

So, how do you receive revelation by faith?

1. Believe God wants to give you revelation.

2. Submit yourself to Holy Spirit.

3. Invite Him to open your understanding and give you revelation.

4. Believe that He will.

5. Expect to receive.

6. Be aware of what is happening in your heart and mind while you wait on Him. "What man is there of you, whom if his son asks bread, will he give him a stone?" (*Matt. 7:9*)

Do we have to "feel spiritual" or "be mature enough" to have experiences in God? No. According to what God says in His Word, all experiences in the Kingdom of God are available to us because of what Jesus has done on the cross. Experience is not dependant on our feelings or how mature we are, but wisdom tells us that we need to be growing in maturity to rightly discern and interpret what we see and hear.

Activating Prayer

Father, I thank You for faith and revelation. I ask that You help me use the faith You have given me to access all You have promised. Help me to walk a life of constantly using and applying my faith to every circumstance. Help me in the area of receiving revelation, to simply believe and access by faith all that You have made available to me. I step into that place of faith and thank You, in advance, for that which You will reveal to me. I look forward with expectation to receiving revelation in new ways. Thank You, Lord, for that revelation and how it draws me closer to You.

5

Spirituality & Revelation

When you start to move among prophetic people and listen to them talk, it is very easy to get overwhelmed by the terms they use and even to misunderstand what they say. It is easy to assume that they see open-eyed visions and have trips to heaven all the time. It is also easy to think that they are somehow more spiritual than you because of the way they talk and what they seem to experience.

So let's kill some sacred cows, some wrong assumptions and beliefs! I don't believe that any particular way of hearing or seeing is necessarily superior to another. Revelation is revelation and no one-way of receiving is more spiritual than another. For example, a thought picture/impression inspired by God can be as weighty and profound as a trance vision.

Likewise, you don't need a higher level of spirituality to hear in particular ways from God; you simply have to be open to receive. In fact, I know some people who are young in the Lord, that regularly see visions and have heavenly encounters. I also know some seemingly very mature Christians, who say they have never had a vision and are still unconvinced that we can even have heavenly encounters today.

Some ways of receiving may be more impressive or dramatic to our natural mind, but that doesn't make them better. All the ways we receive are equally valid. In my walk with God, I have experienced both revelatory impressions and open-eyed visions. While the open-eyed visions are definitely more dramatic to receive, I have sometimes been more deeply impacted by some of the faint impressions I have received from the Lord.

In fact, the God-given subtle impressions and thoughts sometimes require greater faith to walk in than the more dramatic God encounters. Lean into those impressions, chase them down - they often contain deep riches and mysteries.

I remember Patricia King telling us that she has talked to many of the well-known prophets and prophetic people and has asked them, "What is the most common way you get your weighty, heavy duty, Church-changing revelations?" Their answer is very reassuring for all of us. The most common way they receive those weighty revelations is through the still, small voice of God, or the internal visual impression. They all said, they have just learned to embrace what they receive and dig deeper, asking God to open up that revelation further. Wow! How reassuring is that? We all hear like that. Let's capture those faint revelations with our focus and lean into God for deeper insight concerning them.

At the same time, we should desire and ask for all the different ways of receiving revelation to be opened up to us. We are invited to press into God for a greater revelation of Himself and the mysteries of His Kingdom.

There are definitely individuals who move with great ease and sensitivity in the revelatory gifts of the Spirit. Some have unique ministry gifting in those areas, but I believe with faith, practice, and persistence we can all see and hear with greater clarity, and frequency than we do at present.

Some folks might be naturally gifted to play the piano and can even play by ear. Not everyone is blessed in that way but all can learn to play the piano. It is the same with learning to hear from God. We might not all be gifted as prophets but we can all prophesy. We might not all be seers but we can all see.

Levels of Revelation

Some teach that there are levels of revelation and infer that faint impressions are a low level but you can advance to various stages such as "conscious illumination," open visions, trances, and then "in body" and "out of body" trips to heaven.

I believe we can grow in our ability to receive revelation, but that growth is not going from level to level of superiority in vision and experience. The growth is moving into a deeper place of surrender, death to self, and openness to God. It is in pursuing a deeper relationship with Him, so that we know and share His heart more and more. It is being *in Him*, and having Him able to trust us with the secrets of His heart. It is in becoming ever more humbled as we know Him more. In that state of humility, superiority has no place.

I see no indication of these levels in scripture, or of any requirement by God to advance through different levels. Jesus took Peter, James and John into a spiritual encounter where they saw Moses and Elijah. If we subscribe to the idea of levels of revelation, this type of encounter is pretty much up there at the top, yet we do not see evidence of prior levels of revelatory maturity in these three disciples. Saul's encounter with Jesus on the Damascus road in Acts 9:3-9, is another example. As far as we know from scripture, this was his first vision. Yet, if we subscribed to the concept of levels, this would be in the category of open vision or trance. Does it mean that anything these men received after those experiences, which was not on the level of trance vision, was a lesser revelation? Of course not! Yet, according to the idea of levels of experience (meaning, advancing through levels), then anything less would be going backwards.

We cannot command how we receive revelation from God. He is sovereign. He gives the type of revelation that He desires to give. We cannot control that part of receiving revelation. There is no formula that will ensure we receive a particular type of revelation. We simply surrender to Holy Spirit and open our hearts to receive communication and insight from Him.

Fostering the belief that there are superior levels of revelation can create harmful mindsets. Those who have never seen an open-eyed vision may think they are somehow inferior to others who receive the "higher level revelation", or conversely, they might feel superior to others if they experience the "higher levels". God does not have superior or inferior children so let's embrace His unconditional love and walk in humility before Him and each other.

No type of revelation is better than another - they are simply different. The types of revelation you receive, say nothing about you as a person. They say nothing about your character and they are not indicators of maturity or superiority. The revelations you receive simply say you have a loving Heavenly Father, who gives good gifts to His children.

Subjectivity in Revelation

All revelation is prone to subjectivity. Each of us have lenses we look through that distort or color our vision. Our very humanness causes everything we see and experience to be subjective, to one degree or another.

Faint impressions, the still, small voice of God, and some of the other ways of receiving revelation are received through the eyes of our heart (our imagination). As a result, they can be influenced by our thoughts, emotions, doctrinal beliefs, point of view, and even our woundedness. We must be all the more careful in these ways of receiving revelation. Make sure that all things revealed are weighed, judged, and filtered through the knowledge of God's Word, His heart, and His character.

Open-eyed visions, trances and encounters in heaven are also prone to subjectivity. We all filter what we see through personal paradigms, woundedness, values, and our understanding of God's word, heart and character. We must know how to rightly interpret what we are seeing as well as know how to mentor others in what they see and experience.

My husband Rob and I were recently ministering in a nation that is not very welcoming of missionaries. I suddenly had an attack of unstable tummy and had to go to the bathroom. While there, I saw a young child crying. I asked her if she was okay and she asked me to pray with her. She shared that she had just seen a vision of her Dad being arrested by the police. Her father was doing ministry work in this nation. She was scared and thought that because she saw it in a vision that it was definitely going to happen. I shared with her that sometimes God shows us things so we can use the authority He has given us to avert the situation and stop it from happening. We prayed and God's peace filled her. Later, I was able to share with her Mother what had happened. She said her daughter saw visions regularly and that knowing how to mentor her in this gift was at times hard.

This young girl didn't yet have the maturity to understand that not everything God shows us in vision form is a "fait accompli". She saw that revelation through lenses. Those lenses were her age, her understanding of why God gives revelation, and her understanding of God's heart and character. Sometimes God will show us things, like the vision she received, so we will go to prayer and avert the content of the vision from happening.

For some of us, that might be enough to make us say we only want to function in the ways of receiving revelation that are less subjective, but God will not allow that. Why? He wants to partner with us and cause us to grow in our trust in Him. He has not only promised to move sovereignly in our lives, but he has promised to be with us and help us. As we walk by faith in His promises, He goes with us and works in and through us.

Our desire should be to grow in our ability to access all that He has for us. Personally, I want to be experiencing the reality of heaven more and more in my daily life. After all, we are told in Col. 3:1 to "seek those things that are above, where Christ is..."

All that He has and all that He is, has been given to you. Whether you access it or not is up to you. Do you believe it? Use your faith. It's what connects you to the promises of God and enables you to access them.

Activating Prayer

Father, I thank You that you don't require a particular stage of maturity to reveal Yourself to me. Thank You for not playing favorites with your children. Instead, You make everything in your Kingdom available for us to access by faith, as we are in submission to You. I align myself with this truth now and repent of wrong beliefs and assumptions I have had. I position myself in submission to you. By faith, I ask that you will open heaven to me, that I may enjoy the reality of Your Kingdom by revelation and experience. I thank You in advance and expect to receive that which I have asked for. That is Your promise to me in 1 John 5:14-15, "Now this is the confidence that we have in Him, that if we ask anything according to His will, He hears us. And if we know that He hears, whatever we ask, we know that we have the petitions that we have asked of Him." (NKJV)

6

Prophetic Terminology

Some terminology concerning our life in Christ needs to be de-mystified. People need to know exactly what we are saying. We want a Church that is natural and real in its supernatural lifestyle - not weird, spooky or frightening.

There are three extremes we can go to when describing visions and experiences. One can lead to pride, another to a false sense of humility, and the last can lead to deception.

The first extreme is when we love to use the correct terms, but do so in a way that is designed to impress those we are talking to. For example, it can sound impressive to say, "I had a trance vision the other day." It may be true, but we need to be careful that we don't allow spiritual pride to creep in. Pride can defile not only our ability to see and hear but also our delivery. People will sense that defilement around us. While using correct terms, we need to be careful as to how we share and how we describe what we see. We don't want to isolate people or make them feel inferior in any way.

The next extreme is to downplay everything. Because of a

lack of understanding, many modern Christians tend to do this. We either don't understand what we saw, or we say, "I saw a picture" when we mean, "I saw a vision." When we say that, we don't realize we may be downplaying the reality of what happened. We often do this out of a false sense of humility. Don't be afraid to use the word "vision" if you indeed have had a vision. What is the difference between a picture and a vision? I define a picture as something usually static, with no life or movement. A vision, however, is full of the life and power of God, and is often full of movement. Sometimes, you will even see or feel yourself functioning inside that vision.

The last extreme is to exaggerate or stretch the truth. Most of us don't do that deliberately, but we may say things like, "I saw a vision" when we mean that we sensed, perceived, or had an impression. An impression potentially carries as much weight as an open-vision and its reality in the spirit realm is the same. The difference is only in the *receiving* of the revelation. Be careful to make sure you are accurate in how you describe things. Otherwise, you will end up misleading people and in the end you could damage your credibility as well.

There is a balance between the extremes. Use the correct terminology but don't over spiritualize. Don't exaggerate the truth and don't underplay the reality of what you are experiencing.

Manifestations of Revelation

What are some terms prophetic people and scripture use to describe the way revelation is manifested to us? They can sound very mystical and spiritual but let's de-mystify the terms, so we can understand what we are talking about.

The terms listed below are all ways we can receive revelation.

This is not an exhaustive list and the terms are in no particular order, though the first two are the most common ways we receive revelation.

- **Still, small voice of God** -This is an internal hearing. God speaks spontaneous words or thoughts into our mind and heart from our spirit.

- **Internal visual impression** - A thought picture, impression or vision, that is seen with the eyes of our understanding/heart/mind and comes into our mind, or heart from our spirit. Much of what we see in the Spirit will be in the realm of internal sight. It can be initiated by faith in co-operation with the Holy Spirit.

- **Open-eyed vision** - Physical reality fades and the spirit realm is opened before us while our eyes are open. In an open-eyed vision, our spirit usurps our natural body and internal vision center, overriding them.

- **Open-eye spiritual vision** - Our eyes are open but a strong impression, sensing, or perceiving is overlaid onto the physical realm – we can usually still see the physical realm.

- **Closed-eye vision** - We receive a strong impression, or pictures like a TV screen on the back of our eyelids.

- **Trance vision** - Our body usually goes very still and can even be frozen in place. Our eyes can be open or shut. Often we are in the vision, operating within it.

- **Perceiving** - A strong knowing within, that a particular reality is there.

- **The scriptures** - Rhema and logos. Where God makes scripture "come alive" to us. It is usually through thoughts or impressions, but can also be in vision form, when a scripture comes alive to us and we see it as it happened.

- **Through creation** - God shows us revelation through what we see in the natural realm.

- **Dreams / daydreams** - Dreams are often used by God to reveal kingdom mysteries and His heart. They are often symbolic in nature and will often apply to or personal life and emotional state, either conscious or unconscious. Don't dismiss your daydreams. They can often be God speaking into your future.

- **Night visions** - These happen while we sleep but are different from a dream. Night visions are often more literal than symbolic and will often relate to specific situations outside of our personal life.

- **Symbols** - Objects, food, animals, numbers, and nature can all be representative of realities in the heavenly realms.

- **Colors** - In the Word, colors are symbolic and have spiritual meaning.

- **Angelic visitation** - Where we receive revelation from one of God's angelic messengers.

- **Inner audible voice** - When the voice of God is so loud in our mind, it might as well have been audible.

- **Audible voice of God** - God's voice is heard with our natural hearing.

- **Words of knowledge** - One of the gifts of the Spirit, where we know something we could not know naturally about a person or situation.

- **Body impressions** - Through physical sensation - don't dismiss what you feel. For example, heat in the hands often means a healing anointing is manifesting. Pain in the body may be a word of knowledge.

- **Spiritual discernment** - The ability to ascertain the presence, identity, and activities of both good and evil spirits.

- **Inner witness** - God confirms something to you by an inner knowing that "This thing is a God thing."

- **Prophecy** - God speaks to us through other believers. Prophecy is not always accompanied by, "Thus saith the Lord." Mostly it comes in simple, understandable, plain speech.

- **Visitation** - An extended period of time when God speaks through visions or speech to an individual or group, regarding the corporate Body of Christ, a ministry, or individual Church.

Hopefully, the above explanations have helped give understanding to some prophetic terminology. Again, I emphasize the *way* we receive revelation from the Lord is, in the end, not the important thing. The important thing is, we receive revelation and grow in relationship with the Lord and others, as a result. Remember, revelation is revelation however it comes, and all revelation is an invitation to intimacy and co-operation with the Lord.

For Further Study

The Glory School - Patricia King

7

Understanding Revelation

Substance or Reality vs. Concept

When God reveals something to us, we need to ask, "Is this literal or symbolic?" Is this actual spiritual reality or is it *symbolic* of a spiritual reality?

Many things in the Spirit realm have spiritual substance and are reality, not just concepts or ideas. However, not everything we see by the Spirit (in dreams, visions or encounters) will be literal. God often speaks using symbolic language. That is why interpretation of revelation is important. Dream language, in particular, is often symbolic or metaphorical.

Symbolic means:

1. Serving as a symbol: such as a repeating design being symbolic of eternity.

2. Significant purely in terms of what is being represented or implied: e.g., a symbolic gesture.

3. Involving the use of symbols or symbolism: the symbolic meaning of motifs and designs. [1]

Metaphorical means:

1. Something that is regarded as representative, or symbolic of something else. [1]

God often uses parables to speak to His prophets and His people. "I have also spoken [to you] by the prophets and I have multiplied visions [for you] and [have appealed to you] through parables acted out by the prophets." (*Hosea 12:10* Amp)

Much of what God reveals in the Word involves the use of symbolism and parables as illustrations of Heavenly or Kingdom reality. Jesus used parables to share much of what He taught. Parables, as a form of storytelling, are used over 49 times and in a general sense, are seen over 250 times throughout the Old and New Testaments.

But, not everything you see in visions and experiences will be symbolic. Some of it will be reality that exists, either in the natural realm or the spiritual realm. For example, if God shows you a vision of someone you know in a hospital bed and calls you to pray for them (especially if they are actually sick), take note of the details of the room because what you are seeing is quite possibly reality.

An example of seeing spiritual reality happened one day while we were in a conference in Phoenix. During the worship, I had a very strong feeling that there were angels in the room. As I became aware of this, I saw a shimmer out of the corner of my eye, to one side of the stage. In this instance, what I saw was as an open-eyed spiritual vision overlaying the physical realm.

I turned to look and there stood a huge angel-like creature. He was staunch and quite frightening to look at. His clothing was like bright light and he had hands under his wings. But it was his wings that arrested my attention. They were huge and covered with eyes. He stayed in my sight for a few minutes. The more I looked at him, the more I felt convicted of personal and corporate unconfessed sin. Afterward, I searched the scriptures and found that there are definitely heavenly creatures that have wings filled with eyes - they are called "cherubim." So, this is an example of spiritual reality.

We must learn to discern between the symbolic and the actual in the things we see. Knowledge of the Word is a big help. We will often find things we see, written about in scripture. When you experience or see something, ask Holy Spirit if what you are seeing is literal or symbolic. If it's symbolic, ask Him what Kingdom reality it represents. He wants to lead and guide you into truth. If you ask Him, He will tell you.

Here are two examples of symbolic revelations received by students in the Glory Schools we have taught:

- A lady saw the faces of hundreds of babies. They began to move like they were on waves. She couldn't figure it out at first, and then she remembered to ask God questions. When she asked, the vision clarified. She saw humanity woven into the very skin of Jesus - on His hands and in His garments. He was wearing humanity. Obviously, we are not literally woven into the skin of Jesus, but this symbolic picture really confirmed the eternal truth that we are "In Christ."

- Another woman saw a diamond, sparkling and glorious, with light reflecting off it. The diamond was shining and in the hand of God. It was a precious gem, priceless, invaluable, and worth more than gold. She felt it represented the hardness of her faith (faith produced under great pressure). She felt that her trials produced something of incredible value and beauty to the Lord.

Sometimes what the Holy Spirit shows us is spiritual reality and not just symbolic. Jesus gives us some great insights into the realm of spiritual reality. In John 6:63, Jesus says that His words are spirit and they are life – not just concepts. This was brought home to me in a very powerful way one day, when I was sharing with a friend. I was telling her some of the things I had experienced in visions. As I was talking, she began looking around the room. I asked her what she was looking at and she said, "I am looking at your words – I can see them. They have shape and substance, color and weight." Both of us were astounded and we learned something that day: Much of what we think of, as "concept," is real substance in the spirit realm. Every spiritual blessing in heavenly places, as mentioned in Eph 1:3, are substance. They are spiritual reality! In a way our human mind finds hard to comprehend, our words release that substance to do its work.

Jesus proclaimed that He is, "the way, the truth and the life." (John 14:6) The word "truth" in that verse is the Greek word "*alethia*." It not only means truth - but reality. When you embrace truth you are embracing spiritual reality. You can then live in the manifestation of it by co-operating with the Holy Spirit, who leads us and guides us into all truth (reality). Jesus asked of the Father in John 17:17, "Sanctify them by the truth, Your word is truth."

It is also what happens when the Holy Spirit reveals something to us or convicts us. In this case, we interact with the reality of truth, when revealed and then manifest the reality in our life, through our response.

Hebrews 4:12 says, "The word of God is living and active and sharper than any two-edged sword, and piercing as far as the division of soul and spirit... and able to judge the thoughts and intentions of the heart." (NASB)

Don't be afraid to ask the Holy Spirit to make the Word of God come alive to you so that you can interact with the reality of the truth revealed.

Revelation - 3 Parts

Many, when they receive a vision or revelation, make the mistake of believing what they received is the complete communication. But the receiving of revelation or a vision is only the beginning of the process of God speaking. We need to understand the three parts of revelation. These three parts apply to any way of receiving revelation, whether it is seen, heard, felt, etc.

The three parts of revelation are:

1. The revelation itself
2. The interpretation
3. The application

All of these combined together are what make a revelation complete.

The Revelation

This is the actual insight you receive from God through any of the means mentioned previously. Many people make the mistake of stopping at this point. They receive a picture, vision, or a God-thought and think that is all there is to it. The revelation *itself* is just the beginning! It's the start of a wonderful adventure of unravelling a mystery. God does not use mystery to hide things *from* us, but to hide things *for* us. Deut. 29:29 says, "The secret things belong to God but the things revealed belong to us and our children forever." They are only secret because God hasn't revealed them yet.

Those secrets will often be revealed in parable, metaphor, or symbolic form. Our job is to search out the meaning. "It is the glory of God to conceal a thing; but the honor of Kings is to search out a matter" (*Prov. 25:2 KJV*).

We need to be able to interpret what God is saying. This requires relationship. Remember, all revelation is an invitation to intimacy and relationship.

Take note of the overall insight but also the details in it as well. God often hides layers of revelation in a vision or inspired thought. Your revelations can also have a personal and a corporate meaning. Write down the vision or insight in detail – as much as you can remember – so that you can spend time waiting on the interpretation.

Interpretation

The interpretation involves discovering the meaning of the revelation. Make inquiry of God regarding the revelation. Ask Him for details, counsel, and instruction regarding it, lean in to Him for the understanding. Don't be afraid to ask God what a detail means, if it is unclear.

Don't lean to your own understanding to figure out what it means - this is very important! If you go to your head, you will possibly draw a wrong conclusion from your vision. It might not mean what you think it does. Ask the Holy Spirit! He is there to lead you and to guide you into all truth (*John 16:13*).

Ask Holy Spirit specific questions. Ask the *how, why, when, where, what,* type questions. What does this mean? Is this symbolic or literal? Is it for me or for someone else? Is it personal or corporate? What does this symbolize?

Application

The application involves action. "What do I do or how do I respond to the revelation and interpretation?" Every answer to your questions will tell you in greater detail, how, when, etc., to apply what you have seen. Remember to be obedient to what God shows you. This stage of the revelation is extremely important as it discloses the full purpose and intent of the experience. Be sure to follow through.

Let me use a very simple vision of a rose to explain what I mean by revelation, interpretation, and application.

Example:

- **Revelation** of a Rose - Say I get a vision of a red rose that is opening up. I must take note of the details. Is there anything else in the picture? Does the red completely cover the petals? Are there thorns? If so, how many? How open is the rose? Is it an old fashioned rose or a new hothouse type?

- **Interpretation** of Rose Vision - Some questions I could ask: Is this vision for me or for someone else? What does the rose symbolize? Why the color red? What does the color red mean in this instance? Why are the thorns there? What does the opening up of the rose represent?

Often, the answers that God gives you to the questions will lead you to ask Him further questions. Every answer deepens the treasure mined from the revelation.

- **Application** of Rose example - Am I to intercede, to see the vision established without sharing it? Am I to birth it in prayer? Am I to share it? If so, when? Now, or later? Who am I to share it with – a person, a congregation? If I am to share the revelation, what form do I share it in? If I speak it, is it to be done in prayer, decree or prophecy? Is it to be acted out prophetically? Is it to be written? If so, in what form – article, prophetic word form, allegory, parable, poetry, etc.? Is it to be an art piece? If so, what form? Sculpture, painting, sewn as a banner, etc.? Is it to be sung or expressed instrumentally? If sung, is it to be written into a congregational song or a solo, prophetic song?

The depth of mystery that you can mine from a "simple" revelation by asking questions is almost endless. It is, indeed, a grand adventure of discovery when we receive revelation. Every experience potentially reveals more of God to us. In the revealing, we find that we fall more and more in love with Him.

[1] - *New Oxford Dictionary*

8

By Reason of Practice

ractice is valid and scriptural. It is needed to train us in using and developing our gifts. Heb. 5:14 says, "But solid food is for the mature, who because of practice have their senses trained to discern good and evil."

We train our senses through practice. In natural talent and abilities, we practice in order to improve and mature, but often we don't think the same principle applies to the things of God.

Sometimes we feel awkward or nervous at the thought of "practicing" the receiving of revelation and working through the process. Believers can mistakenly confuse their nervousness with spiritual discernment and, as a result, resist the things we should be embracing. We need to learn to discern between the "check" of the Holy Spirit and awkwardness, or nervousness. They are not always the same thing. Often, the uneasy feeling we have is simply the apprehension we feel when trying something new. An uncomfortable feeling itself, does not mean that something is wrong. It can simply mean that it is new and unknown, and we are not yet settled with it.

Most people experience an "awkward" phase when encountering the new and untried. But as we practice, we begin to relax and become comfortable and confident in what we are doing.

I can remember the first time I got behind the wheel of a car to learn to drive. My grandfather was sitting in the passenger seat, telling me what to do. Man, was I nervous and I made mistake after mistake! Did my mistakes and the difficulty of what I was attempting put me off learning to drive? No, they didn't. Not even after I crashed into a power-pole during that first lesson! I pushed through the awkwardness because I wanted the freedom that pushing through would bring me. Now I drive without nervousness and I can go wherever I please, because I pushed through the awkward phase of learning to drive.

If we want to be able to operate in our gifts and Kingdom abilities with freedom and confidence, we must practice them. We must push through the awkwardness to get to the freedom. Remember, our confidence is not in our abilities or our self. Our confidence is in God and His ability to move through our lives. In effect, what we are really practicing when we practice our gifts is simply listening and obeying. The easier we hear and the quicker we obey, the better.

So, take every opportunity you can to practice hearing and discerning. That is how you will grow in the use of your gifts as well as in the understanding of them. Practice them daily. If you don't, they will fall into disuse and you may find it harder and harder to hear God's promptings to use them.

9

Write the Vision

Journaling what we experience in God is important. In Habakkuk 2:2, God encourages the prophet to write out the vision he sees and to make it plain, so that those who read it may run with it.

The Bible is a record of God's relationship with men and women through the ages. It records people's experiences with God, their revelations and interpretations, and in many cases, their applications. It has been given so that we can learn from their life journeys and be instructed with teaching and principles to help us walk out our life with God (*2 Tim. 3:16, 17*).

Journaling the things that God reveals to us and the experiences we have with Him is important for a variety of reasons, some of which are contained in the list below:

- It is all too easy to forget some revelations and experiences as time passes. Journaling helps us to remember clearly.

- Journaling can be used to both record and expand the richness of an experience.

- A journal is a place to create dialogues between yourself and God.

- Journaling helps you to dream, as you record your flow of inspired thoughts and impressions.

- Writing is an act of creating that encourages our understanding and growth.

- Journaling God's words to our heart and our responses to Him can open us to healing and transformation.

- When viewed over time, a journal exposes beliefs and behaviors that limit us.

- A journal serves as a record of emotional and spiritual growth, a testimony of our life.

- A journal is a place to make decisions, cope with change, and gain perspective.

God may well use our experiences with Him to bring encouragement and blessing to others, so that they too, will walk in the reality of the blessings we experience. Our experiences can become a confirmation and invitation for them to experience God at a deeper level and know Him more than they do at present.

A journal is a safe place to record and explore our deepest thoughts as well as our prophetic revelations. It can be used as a place to keep track of our experiences, visions, and prayer requests. We can write poetry, stories, or scripture. We may want to use our journal to write out our thankfulness, hopes, dreams and goals as well as our fears and concerns.

As you follow the process of the activations in this book and journal your experiences, the journal will become a record of your revelations and spiritual growth. In the future, it will jog your memory about things you need to ask greater clarity on, or even revisit.

10

Prophetic Accountability

*C*heck your revelations every so often with a trusted mentor, someone who is mature in their understanding of God, His character, His ways and the scriptures. Without that submission, we can too easily operate outside the boundaries that God has set.

There is no place for lone prophets in the New Covenant. We are part of the Body and "one part cannot say to another, I have no need of you" (*1 Cor. 12:21*). We need to make sure that we are in right relationship with other people and with the Church. Cutting ourselves off from the Church because we are not understood or have been hurt by leadership is a wrong response. It plays straight into the devil's hands, leaving us open to attack and deception.

The submission of our gifts and revelations to others is a safeguard for us and for those we minister to. None of us are immune from mistakes in hearing or interpretation. None of us are perfect, so we need that safeguard.

Submit yourself to the prophetic authority of the Word of God. Confirm that what you see and hear lines up with the nature and character of God, His Word, and His heart. While you might not find exactly what you experience in the Word, ask the Holy Spirit to confirm the validity of what you see or experience through the Word. Ask Him to bring a rhema word to you from scripture, confirming what you have seen. Remember, a valid "God experience" will not violate His principles, Word, heart, or character.

Extra-Biblical Experiences

Although it is important to confirm your revelations through the Word where possible, God can move outside of what is recorded in scripture – not everything God has done is recorded. In John 20:30 & 21:25, we are told that Jesus did many signs in the presence of His disciples that aren't recorded in the Bible.

God will often move in people's lives with experience first and then bring understanding later. Acts 2 is a classic example of this. There are a lot of "firsts" in this chapter, things that the Church had not ever experienced before. In this scripture, the experiences come first then God gives Peter the interpretation, or understanding. Let's look at that passage for a moment.

Acts 2 - The disciples are in the upper room, after being told by Jesus to wait until the Holy Spirit comes. They are praying when, suddenly, a sound like a mighty rushing wind fills the house. Tongues of fire appear on each of them and they begin to speak in tongues. Foreigners heard their own languages being spoken by people who had never learned those languages. Then, three thousand people got saved in one day. These particular phenomena had not been recorded anywhere in scripture prior to Pentecost. These were "firsts" that were outside their theological understanding, until the Spirit of God gave Peter revelatory understanding and he shared that this is what the prophet Joel had talked about.

> "And it will come to pass that I will pour out my Spirit on all flesh; your sons and your daughters shall prophesy, your old men shall dream dreams, your young men will see visions."
> (Joel 2:28)

When you look at what the prophet Joel said, the manifestations Peter and those in the upper room experienced are not mentioned anywhere in that text. But Peter, by the Holy Spirit, saw something in what was happening that connected it to Joel's prophecy. He saw the Spirit of God come on ordinary people and they began to act like prophets. The sign of drunkenness and the prophetic testimony of Jesus, indicated Holy Ghost possession. Then the Holy Spirit quickened those verses to Peter's memory.

There are many other instances in scripture of God moving miraculously in "firsts," when there was no previous scriptural example of that experience. Check out Moses and the burning bush (*Ex. 3:1-6*), Elijah and the boy raised from the dead (*1 Kings 17:17-22*), Elijah carried up in a whirlwind (*2 Kings 2:10-11*), Saul and the light he encountered (*Acts 9*), Gentiles saved and filled with Holy Spirit (*Acts 10*).

You will not find all your encounters outlined in chapter and verse in the scriptures but neither will there ever be a time when a God-experience violates the counsel of scripture. The scriptures will always confirm your encounter in the same way that Joel's prophecy confirmed the outpouring in Acts 2.

Touched, Changed, and Blessed to Be a Blessing

You may have heard the saying, "They are so heavenly minded that they are no earthly good." I believe this statement is one of the most effective bits of demonic propaganda used to discourage people from pursuing heavenly things and the deep mysteries of God. The truth is: the more heavenly minded we become, the more effective on earth we will be.

We cannot see into the eternal realm, experience its reality and be unaffected by it, unless we have a hardened heart. Our experiences with God must be allowed to do their complete work in us, changing us deeply, giving us the Lord's heart and mind, and filling us with His love, compassion, values and character.

The covenant God made with Abraham shows us we are blessed to be a blessing. Any experiences we have should lead us into more co-operation with the Lord in our daily walk, that we might be a blessing to those around us. Having accountability in our lives will help us steward well the experiences we have. It will also keep us from becoming self-focused or going into deception.

For Further Study

Ecstatic Prophecy - Stacey Campbell

11

The Role of the Holy Spirit

*P*art of the Holy Spirit's role is to reveal Jesus, the Father, the heavenly realms, and the mysteries of God. He will lead and guide us into all truth (*John 16:13*). Without the Holy Spirit we cannot have truth revealed to us.

In scripture, we see the Holy Spirit revealed as the One who: [1]

- Leads/Directs - *Matt. 4:1; Mark 1:12; Luke 4:1; 2:27; Rom. 8:14; Acts 8:29*

- Speaks (in, to and through) - *Matt. 10:20; Acts 1:16; 2:4; 13:2; 28:25; Heb. 3:7*

- Casts out devils - *Matt. 12:28*

- Releases power - *Luke 4:14*

- Anoints - *Luke 4:18; Acts 10:38*

- Comes upon/Falls on - *Matt. 3:16; Mark 1:10; Luke 2:25; 3:22; 4:18; John 1:32-33; Acts 10:44; 11:15*

- Baptised/Filled with - *Matt. 3:11; Mark 1:8; Luke 1:15; Luke 1:41, 67; 3:16; 4:1; John 1:33; Acts 4:8, 31; 6:3, 5; 10:47; 2:4; 1:4-5; 7:55; 11:24; 13:9, 52; 1 Cor. 12:13*

- Gives new birth - *John 3:5, 8*

- Leads into worship - *John 4:23*

- Flows like a river from the spirit man - *John 7:38-39*

- Ministers Truth - *John 14:17; 15:26; 16:13*

- Dwells in - *John 14:17; 15:26; 16:13*

- Comforts, heals, and strengthens - *John 15:26; Acts 9:31*

- Proceeds from the Father - *John 15:26*

- Shows us things to come - *John 16:13*

- Gives us the gift of tongues - *Acts 2:4*

- Releases prophecy, dreams, vision - *Acts 2:17-18; 11:28*

- Transports - *Acts 8:39*

- Brings direction, guidance - *Mark 12:36; 13:11; Acts 10:19; 11:12; 21:11; 1 Tim. 4:1*

- Holiness - *Rom. 1:4*

- Spirit of Life, gives Life (ZOE) - *Rom. 8:1, 10*

- Invites us to walk with Him - *Rom. 8:4-5*

- Groans, prayer, intercession - *Rom. 8:26-27*

- Sword (the rhema) - *Eph. 6:17*

- Produces fruit - *Gal. 5:22-23; Eph. 5:9*

- Helps us in weakness - *Rom. 8:26*

- Bears witness - *Acts 5:32; 15:28; 20:23; Rom. 8:15-16; Heb. 10:15; 1 John 4:13; 5:6-8*

- Spirit of adoption - *Rom. 8:15*

- Gives power to mortify the deeds of flesh - *Rom. 8:13*

- Ministers power - signs, wonders, preaching - *Acts 1:8; 1 Cor. 2:4*

- Ministers love - *Rom. 15:30*

- Searches the deep things of God - *1 Cor. 2:10*

- Quickens the mortal body - *Rom. 8:13*

- Brings revelation - *1 Cor. 2:10-12; Eph. 1:17-19; 3:5; Luke 2:25*

- Reveals to us what has been given by God - *1 Cor. 2:12*

- Washes, sanctifies, purifies, justifies - *Rom. 15:16; 1 Cor. 6:11; 2 Thess. 2:13; 1 Tim. 3:16; 1 Peter 1:2, 22*

- Has gifts - *1 Cor. 12:4-11; Heb. 2:4*

- Seals us - *2 Cor. 1:22; Eph. 4:30*

- Liberty - *2 Cor. 3:17*

- Changes us into the image of Christ - *2 Cor. 3:17*

- Promise of the blessing of Abraham - *Gal. 3:14*

- Releases a cry to the Father - *Gal. 4:6*

- Gives access to the Father - *Eph. 2:18*

- Builds us together for a habitation for God - *Eph. 2:22*

- Strengthens us with might - *Eph. 3:16*
- Unity - *Eph. 4:3-4*
- Wine - *Eph. 5:18*
- Supplies - *Phil. 1:19*
- Fellowship - *Phil. 2:1; 2 Cor. 13:14*
- Grace - *Heb. 10:29*
- Glory - *1 Peter 4:14*
- Speaks to the churches - *Rev. 2:11, 17, 29; 3:6, 13, 22*
- Calls for the Bridegroom - *Rev. 22:17*
- Conception of anointings and God's purposes - *Matt. 1:18, 20; Luke 1:35*
- Teaches - *Luke 12:12; John 14:26; 1 Cor. 2:13; 1 John 2:27*

- Gives commandments - *Acts 1:2*
- Power to be a witness (martyr) - *Acts 1:8*
- Boldness - *Acts 4:31*
- Gives sight - *Acts 9:17*
- Commissions - *Acts 13:4*
- Retrains - *Acts 16:6*
- Appoints ministries/Gives authority - *Acts 20:28*
- Releases love - *Rom. 5:5*
- Righteousness, peace, and joy - *Rom. 14:17; 15:13; 1 Thess 1:6*

- Confession of Christ's Lordship - *1 Cor. 12:3*

- Brings the Gospel - *1 Thess. 1:5-6*

- Keeping Power - *2 Tim. 1:14*

- Brings renewal - *Titus 3:5*

- Moves on believers - *2 Peter 1:21*

- Convicts the world - *John 16:8*

We cannot legally enter a spiritual experience without the Holy Spirit as our leader, guide, and safeguard. There are many teachings in the world regarding spiritual experiences and how to have them. The New Age movement is built on this. Many have spiritual experiences without the help of the Holy Spirit. These experiences are real but they are neither legal, or legitimate. Scripture shows many instances of spiritual experiences that were not legitimate or led by the Holy Spirit. These illegal experiences God calls, "witchcraft." Some examples found in scripture are:

- The magician's snakes (*Ex. 7:8-12*)

- The false prophets (*1 Kings 22*)

- King Saul and the witch of Endor (*1 Sam. 28:7*)

- The girl following Paul with a spirit of divination (*Acts 16:16*)

- Simon in Ephesus, who wanted to buy the gift of Holy Spirit and used false signs and wonders (*Acts 8:9-24*)

Develop a good relationship with the Holy Spirit and fellowship with Him. He is not just a servant that you use to do your

71

bidding (i.e. to lead you into an experience of truth.) He is part of the Godhead; inseparable from the Father and the Son. He is a living personality as real as Jesus and the Father.

Thank Him for who He is and what He does for you. Submit yourself to Him and invite Him to lead you through your day. Look for Him during the day. Ask Him what He is doing. Spend time with Him, as you do with your other friends. Acknowledge when you grieve Him and ask His forgiveness. Enjoy His presence and be settled in the peace and rest that He brings.

[1] Glory School Manual with Patricia King, pages 18-21, XP Publishing. All rights reserved. Used by permission of copyright owner.

12

Understanding the Activations

These activations are designed to help you grow in understanding how you see and hear God. Their purpose is to foster and strengthen your relationship with the Father, Son, and Holy Spirit. As you practice the activations, you will discover more of the wonder of who God is and His amazing love for you. The activations are not formulas and they do not have numbered steps that must be followed. The "Process" sections of the activations are to help you unfold the revelations you receive, bringing them out of the realm of mystery into the realm of understanding.

As you continue to practice, you will discover that your ability to see and hear God will become sharper. You will receive more revelation than ever before. The activations aren't anything special, per se, but through them, you are pressing deeper into knowing God.

As you approach the activations, put aside any preconceived ideas of how God will speak to you. The Holy Spirit may show you a picture, speak to you through a God-thought, or even just make you aware of something. Remember, you cannot control the form of revelation but you can position yourself by faith to receive. The Lord will hear and answer. Prophet Bob Jones said, "Anytime you have already formed an opinion about something, you will not be able to hear what the Holy Spirit has to say about it!" He said that when it comes to hearing God clearly, he first has to repent for having an opinion. In order to hear clearly, he must lose his opinion entirely before he can begin to hear God's heart on the subject.

Put aside any preconceived ideas of what you will see. Submit your imagination and your carnal mind to the Holy Spirit. While you can express what you would like to see and experience in your relationship with God, you cannot dictate to Him what you will experience in any activation. Submit yourself to Him and ask Him to lead and guide you.

While you may ask Holy Spirit to show you things relating to the activation, He may choose to do something different that you need to know or experience at that time. However, usually He honors what we ask and shows us things relating to the activation we are doing. When we ask Him for bread He does not give us a stone (*Matt. 7:9-11*). He will always give you revelation, if you ask for it.

How the Activations Are Set Out

The Activation Section gives insight into why you are doing the exercise and what you can hope to glean from it. The Process Section is for you to become accustomed to looking for detail and asking questions. God often hides revelation in details that are seemingly insignificant at first glance. There will often be multiple layers of revelation in an experience. What you get at first look may only be the surface revelation. There are more mysteries waiting to unfold to the hungry, questioning heart. Questions are doorways to understanding our revelations. Don't ever be afraid to ask God questions.

Practice each activation multiple times. God can (and probably will) show you different things each time. But, most importantly, enjoy! Enjoy the process of getting to know God better.

In writing this book and practicing the activations myself, I have grown and learned a great deal. Some I found harder to receive in than others, but that's okay. When you find a particular activation more difficult, continue to practice it. It will become easier and cause you to grow. We are all on a growth journey. We'll spend all of eternity discovering and receiving revelation of the wondrous God we love and serve.

As You Do the Activations

Make sure you set aside enough time for the activation. While revelation can happen in a split-second, we usually need time to receive and process what we see. Remember, these activations are really about relationship and intimacy, not about scoring points or doing an exercise. They are designed to promote dialog with the Lord, furthering your relationship with Him.

As you engage in the activations, bring your body and mind into subjection to your spirit and to the Holy Spirit. The spirit of the prophet is subject to the prophet (*1 Cor. 14:32*).

Taking Thoughts Captive

The Word tells us that we are to bring captive every thought that exalts itself above the knowledge of Christ (*2 Cor. 10:5*). Your mind may try telling you that you are making this up or that this can't really be from God, etc. The devil will certainly try convincing you of this. Your mind can also inject its own agenda and desires into your time of waiting on God. This is why it is important to bring every thought captive to the mind of Christ. We do this by simply declaring it in prayer.

Binding the Demonic

Jesus said that we have the power to bind and to loose in His name (*Matt. 18:8*). Bind the demonic realm from interfering with any part of your time of seeking the Lord.

Invite Holy Spirit to Fill You

Invite the Holy Spirit to fill you with revelation, counsel, insight and understanding. Bring your mind into submission, reminding yourself that you are submitting to the Holy Spirit alone. You have asked Him to show you something, so when it lines up with His word, heart, and character, believe what you see is from Him.

Thanksgiving

Thank Him for everything He reveals to you. Remember, the faintest impression or slightest whisper can carry weighty revelation and life changing power.

I practice these activations myself and get so much out of them every time I do. They introduce me to deeper realms of knowing God. While writing this book, one of the activations I did was "Jesus at work." This is what happened:

I asked the Holy Spirit to show me where Jesus was and what He was doing. I felt that Jesus was sitting on my couch. I couldn't see Him clearly to start with, just a faint swirling and shimmering cloud. I asked the Holy Spirit to make the vision clearer, which He did. I first sensed and then saw that Jesus was writing.

When I asked what He was writing, Jesus said He was writing the inspiration for books yet to be released through me. He further instructed my heart in knowing that the books were reality in the spiritual realm even though they had not yet been made manifest in the natural. He said I needed to make sure that I spent the time needed with Him and to be open to His revelation. He said, "Ask for understanding and experience. Ask for revelation and dig deep into Me. I know everything and I want to lead and guide you into Truth-- into Me. I have made you a voice. I want to release that voice in significant ways - to release truth and experience of Me into the earth and people's lives. I want to stretch you, grow you, and love you into the fullness of expression of all that I have decreed over your life, from the beginning of time. See yourself as I see you. See yourself as heaven sees you. See yourself in all the wonder, greatness, power, and splendor that I have given you. See yourself in humility, recognizing your limitations and faults, but not accepting false boundary lines around your life."

At that point, I felt to go over to the couch and sit beside Him where He continued to speak a number of deeply encouraging personal words to my heart.

I sat there for ages, just pondering and assimilating what He had spoken to me. It was a confirmation to me about this book and what I have felt for ages, regarding my writing. But more than that, it was the call to surrender and humility; the call to go deeper into that place of intimacy with Him that tugged on my heart.

That's what revelation is all about. It's not about the fact that we get a vision or have an experience. It's about what the experience or vision does in us, to bring us into deeper relationship and co-operation with the Lord. Let this be the cry of your heart as you do these activations in His presence. Let it be the deep desire within you and you will find that cry answered.

Following the Activations

Check out what you have seen or heard and line it up with scripture. Dig into the scripture and ask the Lord for a rhema or logos word, confirming what you have seen and experienced. Thank Him for revealing mysteries to you. Write down what you saw, heard or experienced. Take note of details, don't just write a general overview. When writing what you saw, record how you saw it (i.e., as an impression, open-eye vision, trance vision, etc.). Record your emotions and any feelings the experience brings up in you. These can then be talked over and worked through with the Lord after the experience.

No Time and Distance in the Spirit Realm

One reason for journaling your experiences is so you can re-visit them, either by thinking about the experience, or re-entering it in submission to the Holy Spirit.

God's Kingdom operates outside of time and distance. There is no time or distance in the spirit realm. That's why you can be in New Zealand, pray for someone who is in Europe, and see the answer to your prayer manifested in his or her situation. Your prayers transcend time and distance. So it is with spiritual experiences. You can revisit them if you feel there is more to be gleaned from an experience. You simply need to ask the Holy Spirit to take you back into that encounter and He usually will. Your experiences are recorded in your memory bank. The Holy Spirit can lead you right back in through the memory portal. If

He doesn't, you can ask Him and He will tell you why. I often ask the Holy Spirit to revisit an experience. When this happens, I glean even more from the encounter.

One weekend, while teaching at a ladies camp, I shared some things about receiving revelation. As a result, a lady asked the Lord to show her something, which He did. He took her into a heavenly experience right there and then. After the meeting, she approached me with what she had seen and experienced. As she shared, I felt there was more to be revealed to her. I encouraged her to ask the Holy Spirit to take her back into that experience so she could see more. At bedtime, she asked the Holy Spirit to bring further revelation. He took her back into that same encounter and she indeed experienced a whole lot more.

The next day, she rushed up to tell me what had happened. Again, I felt there was still more for her to see. Once again, I encouraged her to ask Holy Spirit to take her back into the experience to gain more insight. He did so, and what He showed her ministered to her on a very deep level, causing her to fall more in love with Jesus than ever. God loves to reveal Himself to us and is more than willing to help us grow in our capacity to receive revelation from Him.

Checklist for Receiving Revelation

1. If you are born again, you are a new creation. You are now "in Christ" and your spirit is sensitive to the Holy Spirit.

2. Have you repented of any known sin? If you haven't, it will cause a separation between you and God. You may not be able to receive pure revelation clearly or be able to ascend easily. "Who may ascend...he who has clean hands and pure heart" (*Ps. 24:3*).

3. Eliminate any other possible voice. You have the authority to bind every demonic spirit from influencing you – deceiving spirits, etc. Bind up and cast down any thoughts that come from the carnal realm, your soul, thoughts, imaginations, and desires. Bind the voice of the world – its mindsets and standards.

4. Submit to the Holy Spirit. He alone can be your guide into heavenly experience and revelation. Any activity in the spirit realm that is not in submission to the Holy Spirit is not only dangerous; it is illegal and an operation of witchcraft (*Deut. 18:10; 2 Chron. 33:6*). He is the Spirit of truth. He will take what is Jesus' and disclose it to you (*John 16:13*).

5. Believe what the Holy Spirit shows you. What He shows you are not just thoughts or concepts - they are the substance/reality of your faith. Either it *is* spiritual reality or symbolizes spiritual reality. James says, "Pray for wisdom in faith. Don't be double minded or you will not receive easily" (*James 1:8*).

6. Yield your body to the Holy Spirit. Bring your body into alignment with the Spirit and what He is doing. Use your body as directed by Him. Sometimes doing something physically will deepen or make more real the experience you are having. For instance, if you are kneeling before the throne of God in Heaven, kneel here in this realm. In this way, your body also enters the spiritual experience in a way it hadn't up until then.

7. No matter how subtle or dramatic, all the experiences the Holy Spirit leads us into are of equal value. Honor what

appears to be seemingly little, as much as the seemingly big. Grab hold of the small and pursue it.

8. Confirm what you receive with the Word of God. Ask the Holy Spirit for confirmation from scripture of what you have experienced. Remember, the Word of God represents tangible reality. It is not just a concept or print on a page. You can enter into that reality.

Now you are ready to proceed with the activations. Have fun and enjoy learning more about the wondrous God who loves you.

13

Activations

A Multi-Faceted God

Activation

*T*here are some who believe that any experience with God in the heavenly realms will be a serious and weighty experience, leaving us so in awe of God that we almost fear to approach Him. Those experiences do happen (especially in the Throne Room) and we should all want them. However, these experiences are an incomplete picture of God. While we should never lose reverence for God, He is much more to us than the Almighty, Awesome, God who is on His throne, arrayed in splendor and majesty.

This activation will help you to see the different ways God chooses to reveal Himself. For example, He reveals Himself in the Word as: Shepherd, Commander, Holy God, Father, Creator, King, the One who sits on the Throne, the God who laughs in the heavens, as well as many other revelations in scripture. Jesus is revealed as Bridegroom, Lion of Judah, and more. Some of the

Holy Spirit's manifestations are: breath, wind, fire, and oil.

God understands when we have difficulty relating to some aspects of His nature, but He wants us to be free to respond in an unhindered way, however He reveals Himself. This exercise will help you become familiar with Him and respond to Him with trust and freedom.

Do this activation for each of the facets of His nature listed above and any others God shows you in the Word.

Process

Ask these questions of the Holy Spirit and be sure to write the details of all you see and hear.

- Ask the Lord to give you a vision of Him as one of the above, e.g. Shepherd, Commander, Bridegroom, etc. Describe what you see.

- What is He wearing?

- What is He is doing? Remember, the details are important.

- Ask Him why He revealed that aspect of who He is to you. Write what you hear.

- Ask Him to show you any areas you have difficulty relating to this aspect of who He is and why? What is He showing you?

- Repent, if you need to, for not trusting Him in this area. Ask Him to heal any wounds that prevent trust from developing to its fullest.

- How does He want this revelation to be established in your life, bringing change?

- How are you to incorporate this revelation of Him into your life - Study, decree, soaking, worship, etc?

- How does the Lord desire to reveal this aspect of Himself to the Church?

- Ask Him how you can release this revelation – e.g. through intercession, decree (written or spoken), prophetic word, worship, symbolic or prophetic act? Record your impressions.

The Father

Activation

This activation will help develop your relationship with God as your Heavenly Father. "We have received the spirit of sonship and adoption. We are no longer orphans, but beloved children of the Lord." (*Rom. 8:15*)

In this activation, you will feel His heart for you and know in a greater way, the reality of that relationship. Don't try to write anything down in the beginning; just enjoy being with Him and let the revelation unfold. Remember, it's about relationship, not just performing an exercise.

Process

Ask these questions of the Holy Spirit and be sure to write the details of all you see and hear.

- Ask the Holy Spirit to reveal God to you as Father.

- What would the Lord like to reveal about Himself, as your Father?

- Let Him minister to you in whatever way He desires. Take time and just allow Him to love you.

- Ask Him how you can cooperate with Him in what He is doing. Describe your impressions.

- How does He see you? What is in His heart for you? Ask Him to tell you one thing He likes about you. What did you hear?

- Ask Him how you can have His heart for yourself. Record what you hear or sense.

- Take note of the following and later, write down what you noticed.

- Explore these details, as they will reveal where you are in relationship with Him. When you first entered the experience, where was Father? Was He in the room with you? Was He somewhere else?

- Where in that place/room were you, in relation to Him? What were you doing there? Write the details of all you sense or hear.

- What were your initial feelings, after you first entered into the experience? Record them, using feeling words such as: I felt vulnerable, safe, distant, etc.

Jesus at Work

Activation

Jesus is at work both in you and around you. This activation gives you insight into how you can co-operate with Him in what He is doing.

Process

Ask these questions of the Holy Spirit and be sure to write the details of all you see and hear.

- Ask the Holy Spirit to show you Jesus. He may do so in vision, with words, or in any of the ways we have discussed. Where is He? Is He in the room with you? Write all that you see and hear.

- What clothes He is wearing? Note the colors, style, etc. Are the clothes task-oriented or position-oriented? Ask Him why He is dressed in this way.

- What is He doing? Take note of details, such as: is He is sitting or standing near someone? Is He is facing toward them or away from them? Is He facing a certain direction, etc?

- Ask Jesus why He is there. Write down what you hear.

- Inquire if there is any way you can work together with Him in what He's doing, at this time. Write down what He says or what you sense.

- If Jesus is near someone, ask Him to share His heart for that person with you. Write down what He says. Be descriptive. Use feeling words that express His heart, if possible. If the emotions are negative in any way (e.g.

sadness), try and find a positive way to express that. In other words, what is the positive thing Jesus wants to do in their life (e.g. give them a garment of praise for a spirit of heaviness)?

- Now that you know His heart for that person, ask Him how you can know the same love He has for them. What did you hear?

- If that person is you, ask Him what ways you unconsciously work against knowing His love?

- If Jesus is showing you His heart for someone, ask if you should share what He has shown you with him or her. If so, how should it be shared?

Walking With the Holy Spirit

Activation

This activation will help you realize that the Holy Spirit walks with you. It will bring understanding of His function and how you can cooperate with Him.

The Holy Spirit is within us but also with us in this world. He longs to work *with* us, revealing Jesus and the Father *to* us and *through* us to others.

Process

Ask these questions of the Holy Spirit and be sure to write the details of all you see and hear.

- Ask Holy Spirit where He would like to take you for a walk.

- Where are you? Describe the details of all you see.

- What is the Holy Spirit doing?

- Ask the Holy Spirit why He is taking you there. What did He say?

- Ask Him how you can cooperate with what He is doing.

- If there are other people in the vision, ask what His heart is for the person He is standing closest too. This might be you.

- Ask Him how you can have the same heart for this person, even if it is you. Describe all that you sense and hear.

Surprise Me

Activation

God loves spontaneity and surprises. He loves revealing who He is to us, and enjoys it when we allow Him to surprise us with revelation and love. Some of us gravitate to one type of encounter or way of receiving revelation, because that is where we feel comfortable. This exercise will help stretch you further out of your comfort zone. Practice this activation often and allow God to expand your capacity to receive.

Process

Ask these questions of the Holy Spirit and be sure to write the details of all you see and hear.

- Ask Holy Spirit to surprise you and give you revelation in whatever way He desires. It may be something you see or hear; it may come in any of the ways we have described throughout this book.

- If He has taken you somewhere, describe where you are.

- Ask the Lord why He is showing you this revelation. What is He saying?

- Ask for clarity in interpretation and application, if applicable. Record what He tells you.

- Ask how you can cooperate with what He is doing. Describe your impressions.

Words of Knowledge

Activation

This activation will help develop your ability to hear words of knowledge and develop trust in the Holy Spirit's ability to guide you into truth and revelation.

Process

Ask these questions of the Holy Spirit and be sure to write the details of all you see and hear.

- Ask the Lord for a word of knowledge, regarding someone you know. It may be in any area, such as physical, emotional, financial, etc.

- A word of knowledge may reveal itself in one of several ways. You may hear the still, small voice of God, get body sensations (like pain or heat), or see a vision or impression in the imagination (sometimes of part of the person's body or a circumstance).

- If you get a generalized answer, ask for more detail. Remember, questions mine the treasure in a revelation. Write down what you hear.

- Connect with the person and have a conversation with them. During your conversation, slip in the word of knowledge you received. Ask them if they can relate to it in any way. If they question what you are doing, explain that you are practicing how to step out in a word of knowledge.

- If they can't relate to the word you received, talk with them more. See if you can find out where you were off in what you heard.

For example, one time I felt that there was sickness around a woman's life. I assumed she was the one who was ill. It turned out that she wasn't sick, but her sister was facing a major battle with cancer. The word of knowledge was correct; I just didn't ask the Lord enough questions to get the right details.

- Do the same activation tomorrow at work. Ask Holy Spirit for a word of knowledge, regarding someone you work with.

- Practice the activation at church this week.

- Do the same activation in the supermarket, at the checkout.

- This exercise can be done anywhere, anytime.

Scripture References

You can also do this activation regarding scripture passages.

Ask Holy Spirit for a scripture reference. Don't look it up, yet. Ask for detail about that passage.

- Ask for personal insight for your life, regarding the passage. Note what the Lord shows you.

- Now, go and check out the passage, see if you were right! If what you felt isn't an actual verse, just do the exercise again. Don't get discouraged. Remember, it is all about learning to hear and trust, not about keeping score. I'm sure you received some good revelation from the Lord, even if you got the actual reference wrong.

Envisaging the Reality of the Word

Activation

God has always spoken through His Word. He still speaks to us through the Bible in dynamic, living ways today. In this activation, we are asking God to give us revelation of those things contained in His living and active Word. He loves to give us revelation and talk to us about His eternal Word.

This exercise will help you gain fresh insight into the Bible. It will help expand your understanding of there being no time or distance in the spirit realm. God operates beyond time, as we know it.

Process

Ask these questions of the Holy Spirit and be sure to write the details of all you see and hear.

- Ask the Lord to give you a passage of scripture - book, chapter and verse(s).

- Look at the passage. If it's a passage describing a place or event, ask the Lord to show it to you visually. Describe what you see or experience, in detail.

- Note what sort of vision it is. Are you seeing the vision from the outside or inside? What are you feeling, smelling and hearing? What is happening? Is it a thought impression, open-eyed vision, closed-eye vision, etc? Record how you are seeing it.

- If it is a descriptive passage, ask questions like, "What size was that?" or "What color was that?" Ask the exploratory questions (how, why, where, when and what). Questions lead to more revelation.

- Don't just take a cursory glance at the situation, look for the details. Record anything you missed in your first glimpse of the vision.

- Ask the Lord for personal insight into the scripture and how you can apply that insight. Journal what you hear.

- Ask the Holy Spirit for corporate insight into the scripture and how you can apply/release that insight. Write anything you hear.

Fruit of the Spirit

Activation

This activation will draw your attention to the fruit of the Spirit being grown and developed in your life.

The fruit of the Spirit involves the manifestations of God's character and nature in your life. The growth and development of fruit is a product of environment and the choices you make to co-operate with Holy Spirit. He develops the fruit in your life. The fruit of the Spirit is like any fruit; it gives sustenance, causing growth and development to the partaker.

Process

Ask these questions of the Holy Spirit and be sure to write the details of all you see and hear.

- Ask the Lord to show you the spiritual reality of one of the fruits of the Holy Spirit: love, joy, peace, patience, kindness, goodness, faithfulness, gentleness, and self-control.

- Does that fruit have a visual manifestation? Describe its appearance, including shape, color, size, texture, etc.

- Does it have a fragrance? How does it smell?

- Is there a sense of taste that comes to you? Describe the taste.

- Ask the Lord how the fruit affects your life. What do you hear?

- Ask the Lord if there are ways you could develop this fruit further in your life.

- What would He have you do to encourage and tend its growth in your life?

- Are there any angels that minister growth of this fruit? Ask Him how they minister it in your life and the lives of others. Journal all that you see and hear.

Crowns

Activation

The Bible speaks of many different crowns that we wear. Your life is likened to a crown of beauty in the hand of the Lord (Is. 62:3).

Other crowns include:

An imperishable crown

A crown of righteousness

The crown of life

The crown of glory

Golden crowns

You are crowned with glory, honor, and knowledge.

You are crowned with loving kindness and compassion.

"I am coming quickly, hold fast to what you have, so that no one will take your crown" (*Rev. 3:11*).

Crowns can be lost. We can give them away by our life and actions. We are charged with protecting our crowns.

There can also be symbolic visions of crowns. A few years ago, I had a vision in which God showed me types of headwear that we substitute for the crowns we should be wearing. This particular vision related to worship.

Process

Ask these questions of the Holy Spirit and be sure to write the details of all you see and hear.

- Ask Holy Spirit to show you a vision of a crown. What do you see? What is it made of; any gemstones or patterns, etc?

- Ask Him what the crown is. What is its meaning and symbolism? Record all He says.

- Who is the crown for? Why is the Lord giving them this crown? What are your impressions?

- What is the cost on the life of the one wearing and keeping hold of the crown?

- If the crown is yours, ask if you can experience wearing it. Describe what it feels like. What emotions are you feeling? Does it make you see yourself any differently?

Trees & Their Fruit

Activation

In many places, the Bible speaks of our lives producing fruit (*John 15:8*). It also refers to us being like trees planted by water (*Ps 1:3*). This activation will draw your attention to the good and bad fruit being grown in your life and surrounding spiritual environment.

The term "fruit" is used to describe what is produced in our life and environment. A tree has to be in an environment that is conducive to growth and it has to be cared for. The tree's fruit is a product of its natural or spiritual environment. It could be a manifestation of the Tree of Life, or a manifestation of the Tree of Knowledge of Good and Evil. Fruit trees have been in the center of human life since the garden. Some trees you need to tend and others you need to cut down.

Process

Ask these questions of the Holy Spirit and be sure to write the details of all you see and hear.

- Ask Holy Spirit to allow you to see where you are in the spirit realm and to show you a tree, symbolizing what is happening there. Describe what it looks like, where it is, and its size.

- What are its surroundings? Is the tree wild or cultivated? What type of soil is it in? Can you see its roots? Are they healthy? Write down all the details.

- Is there fruit on the tree? If so, describe its appearance, including the type, shape, color, size and ripeness.

- Can you smell the fruit? If not, ask the Lord to give you a sense of its smell. Describe it. Does the smell cause any physical or emotional reactions? Does it stir any memories, e.g. remind you of a particular time in your life or time of year?

- Ask the Lord if the fruit is edible and what affect it will have if it's eaten. Is it fruit you are allowed to eat? If yes, partake! Record its taste and if it has any affect on you. Is it sweet, bitter, etc?

- A tree comes from somewhere. Ask the Lord who planted it and who looks after it. Look for any gardeners, people, or creatures nearby. Describe what you see and hear.

- Ask the Lord if there is anything that this tree needs to be stronger, healthier, and more productive.

- If it is to be removed, how do you remove it?

Feasts & Banquets

Activation

Scripture speaks of feasts and banquets the Lord prepares for us. Among those feasts, we find a table prepared in the midst of our enemies and the marriage supper of the Lamb. Many feasts were instituted just to show Israel different aspects of God. Often, in heavenly experiences, people see banqueting tables and sit to eat with the Lord and others.

Process

Ask these questions of the Holy Spirit and be sure to write the details of all you see and hear.

- Ask Holy Spirit to show you a feast or banquet, taking place either on Earth or in Heaven. Describe where you are and what you see.

- As always, take note of details. What kind of place settings are there and for how many? Is the table fully or partly set? Is there food on the table? If so, what sort?

- Is the feast for you or for others? If for others, then whom?

- What is the significance of the feast?

- Is there a protocol or requirements for those invited to partake?

- Take note of any people. What are they wearing and what are they doing?

- Describe what are you wearing? Are you dressed appropriately? If not, ask Holy Spirit what you should be wearing. Ask if you need to provide the garment or if the Lord supplies it. Record all that is said and done.

Spiritual Clothing

Activation

In Ephesians 6, we see that what we wear can represent equipping and preparation. This activation will help you understand how you and others are being equipped and prepared.

Process

Ask these questions of the Holy Spirit and be sure to write the details of all you see and hear.

- Ask the Lord to show you an outfit of clothing. Include any colors and design features, as you journal what you see.

- Why are the clothes being worn? Do they have a function (task oriented or position oriented)? What did Holy Spirit reply?

- Describe any accessories with the outfit. What is their function?

- Are the clothes for you or someone else? Are they for an individual or for a group? Write all that you hear.

- Why is the Lord giving the clothes to this person? Ask the Lord if the clothes come with a cost. If so, what is the cost?

- Ask the Lord the consequences/fruit/significance of wearing the clothing. Record all you hear or sense.

People

Activation

This will help you see the ways God is at work in the lives of those around you. You will see how they are being equipped and prepared for life and service.

God wants us to be aware of His plans and purposes for the lives around us. We are blessed to be a blessing. To be a blessing, we need to be able to see and identify needs.

Process

Ask these questions of the Holy Spirit and be sure to write the details of all you see and hear.

- Ask the Lord to show you a person. It may be someone you do or don't know. Who do you see?

- Is this is an actual person or a representation of a certain group of people?

- What are they wearing. What do the clothes mean? What is their function, etc?

- Ask the Lord: Why have You shown me this person? What do You want to do in their life?

- What would You like me to do with what You have shown me? Would You like me to pray, prophesy, write a word of encouragement, etc?

- Spend time praying for this person. Use faith-filled prayers and decree the positive that God desires for them. Don't come into agreement or reinforce anything negative.

Burdens & Baggage

Activation

We all carry burdens and excess baggage in our lives at times. God wants to deal with those things. If it is not ours to carry, we can hand the burden over to Him. We don't always realize that we are carrying baggage we shouldn't, until He shows us. Other times, He may give us a prophetic burden or a burden to be carried in intercession, until birthed and released.

This activation will help you recognize the burdens and/or excess baggage that you or others carry. It will help you distinguish between different types of burdens.

Process

Ask these questions of the Holy Spirit and be sure to write the details of all you see and hear.

- Ask the Lord to show you a burden in whatever shape He chooses. What is He showing you? What is the substance, density, shape, size, and texture. Is the color clean or dirty, clear or clouded?

- Is it a burden related to you? If so, where are you in the picture? What are you doing?

- Is the burden related to someone else? If so, whom?

- Is this burden from the Lord, the enemy; or from your own misunderstanding, sin, or ignorance?

- Ask the Lord what it represents. What did He say?

- Is there a feeling that comes to you along with this picture? Describe that feeling.

- What does He want you to do with this burden? Record your impressions, any symbolic actions, etc.

- What would the Lord like you to learn from this?

- Is there any action He wants you to take? If the burden is from the demonic realm, bind it, in Jesus' name. Command it to go; get rid of it! Ask the Lord for further instruction on how to obtain freedom from it.

- If it is a burden from Jesus, how would He like you to proceed? Are you to release it, intercede, decree, prophesy, or perform any symbolic action?

Nations & People Groups

Activation

Psalm 2:8 tells us that the nations and their people are a part of our inheritance. We are to ask God for them. Do some research in the Word to discover how we are connected to the nations. You may have personal or corporate connections to a specific nation. God will give you His heart for them. This activation will help develop your heart for the nations.

Process

Ask these questions of the Holy Spirit and be sure to write the details of all you see and hear.

- Ask the Lord to show you a nation.
- Ask the Lord to show you something about that nation. What is He showing you?
- What is that nation's prophetic destiny? What things come to your natural mind about that nation? Do the two line up with each other? Record your impressions.
- Ask if the nation has any personal significance for your life?
- What does the Lord want you to learn and do from this? Are you to intercede for this nation? Are you to go to it at some stage? Are you to keep track of it in the news, etc? If so, what does God want you to be watching for?
- Ask God to give you prophetic insight into that nation's state and the strategy to pray for it.
- Do this exercise again with the nation of Israel in mind. Israel has an end time purpose and destiny and we are all linked with that.

Animals

Activation

Animals can have spiritual significance and meaning. I encourage you to do some research. Study the animals in the Bible and those you see in your visions. God provides many life lessons through animals.

This activation will help develop your understanding of the way God speaks through animals, nature, etc.

Process

Ask Holy Spirit the following questions. Be sure to write, in detail, all that you see and hear.

- Ask the Lord to show you an animal. What do you see? What is its appearance, shape, and size?
- Is the animal clean or dirty? Healthy or unhealthy?
- Is the animal interacting with anything? What is it doing?
- What comes to mind as you think of that animal? What is your natural understanding of what that animal represents?
- Ask if it represents the same in the spiritual realm. Record your impressions.
- Ask if the animal has any personal significance for your life?
- Ask the Lord if there are life lessons for you to learn from it?
- What does He wants you to do as a result of this encounter? Is there an area you need to repent, an area of healing, or an area to intercede, etc?

Objects

Activation

This activation will develop your understanding of the way God speaks through objects.

Objects can have spiritual significance and meaning. Do research in the Word to find out about the objects you see in your visions. God provides many life lessons through them.

Process

Ask Holy Spirit the following questions and write in detail, all that you see and hear.

- Ask the Lord to show you an object and describe what you see. What is its appearance, shape, and size?

- Is the object clean or dirty?

- What comes to mind as you think of that object? What is your natural understanding of what that object represents?

- Ask the Lord if it represents the same in the spiritual realm. Record your impressions.

- Ask Him if the object has any personal significance for your life? What did He say?

- Are there life lessons for you to learn from it?

- What would He like you to do as a result of this experience? Is there an area in which you need to repent, an area of healing, or an area to intercede, etc?

- Does the object have any corporate significance for a group you are a part of? What are your impressions?

- Write down what you have seen, so that you don't forget it. Also, writing it down will remind you of your account-ability to God to do what He has asked of you.

Colors

Activation

Colors have spiritual significance and meaning. Do research, in the Word or study guides, to find out about the colors you see. It is important we learn how to correctly recognize and interpret those things we see in the Spirit. This activation will help de-velop your understanding of the symbolism of colors.

Process

Ask Holy Spirit the following questions and write, in detail, all that you see and hear.

- Ask the Lord to show you a color.

- What do you see? What is its substance, density, shape, size, and texture? Is the color clean or dirty, clear or clouded?

- Is it a color you recognize? If so, what is your natural understanding of what the color represents?

- Ask the Lord if it represents the same in the spiritual realm. Record your impressions.

- Is there a sense of taste that comes to you along with this color? What does it tastes like?

- Ask Him if the color has any personal significance for

your life, a geographical area, a circumstance, or someone else's life? What did He say?

- What does the Lord want you to learn from this? What would He like you to do, as a result of seeing and experiencing this color?

Portals, Windows, Doors & Gates

Activation

The Word talks about the windows and gates of Heaven. This implies that there is more than one window and more than one gate in Heaven. The different gates to Jerusalem all had different names with different meanings. Earthly Jerusalem is a representation of the heavenly Jerusalem, so its gates have different names and meanings too.

Portals, entranceways, and gates, come in many shapes, sizes, and forms. Jacob saw a ladder that he called the "gate of heaven." Jesus became a portal upon which angels ascended and descended. This activation will help you become aware of the windows, portals, gates, or doors in the spirit realm.

Process

Ask these questions of the Holy Spirit and write in detail all that you see and hear.

- Ask Holy Spirit to show you a heavenly window or portal. Describe, in detail, what you see.

- Is the portal open or shut? Ask Him, "Why?"

- Ask Him where the portal leads. Record your impressions.

- What is the function of this portal - what goes in it and what comes through?

- Ask if it is a portal that you may enter.

- Is there a protocol to enter? What do you hear Holy Spirit saying?

- If He gives you permission, go ahead and enter. Describe all you see and hear. Take note of the details and what they may symbolize.

Discerning of Spirits & Spiritual Beings

Activation

We live in a spiritual world as well as the physical world. The spiritual realm is inhabited by spiritual beings that also work within the physical realm. Even if we are unaware, we are constantly interacting with the spirit world. If we ask, God will open our eyes to that realm. Scripture speaks to us about the "discerning of spirits." This gift is to help us know with whom we are interacting and whom they serve. If we are to interact with spiritual beings, we have to grow in the discernment of spirits.

This activation will make you aware of the spiritual beings around you; both in this earthly environment and in the heavenly realms – angels, demons, beasts, elders, cloud of witnesses, living beings, seraphim, cherubim, horses, etc.

Process

Ask these questions of the Holy Spirit and write in detail all that you see and hear.

- Ask the Lord to show you a spiritual being that is in the location or room where you are. Describe that being, what it looks like and where it is. Look closely at it. Check for features like wings and other things. Describe what you see and where.

- Ask the Lord if this spiritual being is from Him or from the enemy. Describe your impressions and what you hear.

- Ask the Lord what it is doing and why it is there. What is your impression?

- What is it wearing? Look at colors, patterns and type of clothing. Describe them.

- Is it carrying any objects or are there any near it - things like weapons, bags, musical instruments, etc.? Describe the objects.

- If it is a messenger from God, ask if he/she/it has any message from God for you. It may have a prophetic insight or impartation for you. Record any conversation or interaction that occurs between you.

- If it is demonic in origin, command it to leave, in the name of Jesus. Write down what happens.

Spiritual Senses

Activation

Our spirit man has the same senses as our natural man: sight, hearing, taste, touch, and smell. We need to learn how to recognize and interpret those things we see, smell, feel, hear, and taste in the Spirit. Some people will find certain senses are better developed than others. They can all be developed with time and practice and we should seek to do so. This activation will draw to your attention and help develop your other spiritual senses. Repeat this activation with taste, touch, and hearing.

Process

Ask these questions of the Holy Spirit and be sure to write the details of all you see and hear.

- Ask the Lord to awaken your sense of smell in the spirit.
- Describe the fragrance you can sense – you may smell it in the natural realm or you may sense the fragrance in the spiritual realm.
- Does the fragrance remind you of anything?
- Is there a sense of taste that comes to you? What does it taste like?
- Is the smell pleasant or unpleasant? Is it from the Lord, the world, or the demonic realm?
- Is there a sense of color that comes with the fragrance? Describe the color, shape, texture, etc
- Ask the Lord what the fragrance is.

- Is the fragrance associated with your life, a geographical area, an object, or someone else's life? Record your impressions.

- Ask the Lord what He wants you to learn from this? What would He like you to do as a result of encountering this fragrance?

- If it is from the demonic realm, what is it associated with? Bind it, in Jesus name and command it to go. Ask the Holy Spirit for more insight on dealing with it.

The Throne Room

Activation

The Word tells us we are seated with Christ, in Heavenly places and that Christ is seated at the right hand of the Father, on high. The Throne Room is a literal place in the Third Heaven. We are told that we can boldly come to the Throne of Grace anytime. We have access to the Throne 24 hours a day, 7 days a week. The invitation has already been extended; we just need to accept it. In this activation, you will access His invitation and experience the reality of the Throne Room.

There are many wonders here! You may see the sea of glass, like crystal; the river that comes from the base of the throne; rainbows, like emerald around the throne; people, angels, living creatures, etc. All these wonders are part of our inheritance to experience and enjoy. Be aware, you may not see everything in one visit; sometimes, you will catch glimpses or just see a part of an area.

Process

Ask these questions of the Holy Spirit and be sure to write the details of all you see and hear.

- Ask the Lord to show you/take you to the Throne Room. Describe the details of all that you see and hear.

- Where are you? Are you inside the Throne Room or at the entrance? If you're at the entrance, ask why you are standing there. What did the Lord say?

- Ask if there is a protocol for entering. If so, what is it?

- How much of the throne room can you see? Describe what you see, but don't guess at what else may be there.

- Where is the Father? Where in that place/room are you in relation to Him? What is He doing?

- Where is Jesus? Where in that place/room are you in relation to Him? What is He wearing? Describe what He is doing or saying.

- Is the Holy Spirit there? What is He doing?

- What other people or creatures do you see? Describe them and what they are doing.

Heavenly Places

Activation

The Bible speaks of many different things in Heaven: the river, mansions, gates, etc. People who have been to Heaven, report on other places also such as: counsel rooms, the library, gardens, warehouses with body parts, and the treasury. Are these literal places or symbolic? We don't know for sure, but we do know that God uses visions of places to teach us and show us spiritual realities. This activation will help you become aware of the heavenly realms and the different places in Heaven.

Process

Ask these questions of the Holy Spirit and be sure to write the details of all you see and hear.

- Ask The Holy Spirit to show you a heavenly place. Describe what you see. Remember, details are treasure!

- Ask if this place is real or if it's a symbolic picture.

- Does this place have a function? What is it used for?

- Ask if it is a place that you may enter. Record what you hear.

- Is there a protocol for entering? If so, what are your instructions?

- Go ahead and enter, if He gives you permission. Describe what you see and hear. Take note of the details and symbolism.

Worship In Heaven

Activation

Heaven and the Throne Room are filled with worship! Everyone and everything there, worships God. Scripture relates many descriptions of the worship in Heaven. Because you are a child of God in Christ and seated with Him in Heavenly Places, you can experience the reality of that worship! This activation will help you experience and participate in Heaven's worship.

Process

Ask these questions of the Holy Spirit and be sure to write the details of all you see and hear.

- Ask Holy Spirit to help you access the Throne Room or Heavenly Places, to experience the worship there. Describe all you see and hear.

- Who do you see there? Ask who they are.

- If they are doing something, ask what the symbolism is in their actions.

- Ask if you can join in.

- What does it feel like to worship there? What were you doing as you worshipped?

- Describe what you see there: the sounds, sights, smells, etc., of Heaven's worship.

Prayer & Intercession - In Heaven

Activation

Scripture teaches that there are angels in Heaven, who hold harps and golden bowls of incense in their hands (*Rev. 5:8*). These are the prayers of the saints. There is intercession in Heaven. Jesus ever lives to make intercession for us. He is our intercessor, who gives us right of access to the Father and the Throne of Grace. Is it possible for us to hear the intercession of Heaven and join in? Let's find out with this activation.

Process

Ask these questions of the Holy Spirit and write the details of all you see and hear.

- Ask the Lord to help you access the Throne Room. What do you see and hear?

- Ask Him if you can hear the intercession of Heaven. Record what He says and what He shows you.

- Describe any people or heavenly creatures you see. What are they saying? What symbolic or prophetic actions are they doing?

- Look for Jesus, who is our living intercessor. What is He doing or saying? Write down what you see and hear.

- Ask if you can join in with the intercession. Describe what the Holy Spirit says and what you feel to do and say in that intercession.

- How does the Lord want you to release Heaven into Earth, so that His Kingdom might come on Earth, as it is in Heaven? Write down any prophetic or symbolic actions He asks you to do. Record any decrees that He asks you to make.

- Obey what He says. Do the actions and make the decrees, knowing that whatever you ask for in faith, believing you have received, you shall have!

Heavenly Transportation

Activation

This activation will help develop your understanding of spiritual/heavenly transportation.

The Word speaks of different modes of transportation in the spirit. We see examples of it in Jesus life (*Matt. 14:25; John 6:21*), heavenly chariots (*2 Kings 2:12*), physical transportation of your body, from one place to another (*Acts 8:39-40*), rising up or flying with wings like eagles (*Is. 40:31*), as well as other heavenly transport (*2 Kings 5:26; Ps. 18:10; Col. 2:5; Rev. 12:14; 19:14*).

In the days ahead, we will need to appropriate some of these transport modes to accomplish what God has called us to do. Therefore, we need to understand what they are and how to access them as Holy Spirit leads us.

Process

Ask these questions of the Holy Spirit and write the details of all you see and hear.

- Ask the Lord to show you a mode of heavenly transportation. Describe what you see.

- Ask why He showed you this particular mode of transport. What significance does it have? What significance does it have for you this very moment? Record your impressions.

- Ask Him if you can experience it. If He says, "Not at this time," don't be disappointed, but be thankful. Praise Him for it!

- If He says, "Yes," ask Him if you can go somewhere now.

- Ask Him where He wants to take you and why?

- Describe what you see and what you experience.

- Was it a fun trip introducing you to Father's love or a ministry assignment? What did you learn from this experience?

Every Spiritual Blessing

Activation

In Ephesians 1:3, we find that we have been blessed with every spiritual blessing in the heavenly places. We need to know what those blessings are and how to release them from the spiritual realm into the natural. This activation will help you identify those blessings, apprehend them, and release them.

Process

Ask these questions of the Holy Spirit and write the details of all you see and hear.

- Ask the Lord to show you the reality (or spiritual substance) of the spiritual blessings in Ephesians 1. Describe what you see – appearance, shapes, sizes, colors.

- Ask the Lord to help you recognize what the blessings are as you see them. Ask Him to highlight one to you.

- What is that spiritual blessing? Name it and describe it. What do you see?

- What comes to mind as you think of that blessing? What is your understanding of what that blessing represents?

- Ask Him if your thoughts about it are correct or if they need adjusting. If they need adjusting, ask Him to do so. Ask for revelation on that blessing and record what He shows you.

- Why did the Lord reveal this particular blessing to you?

- Ask the Lord if there are lessons for you to learn from this revelation. What does He want you to do as a result of this? Is there an area that you need to step into in a new way? Do you need to take ownership or release it? Ask Him and record what He shows you.

- How are you to bring this blessing from the spiritual, into the natural and release it? (e.g., intercession, decree, prophetic word, symbolic, or prophetic act?) Record your impressions.

14

Prophetic Symbols, Colors & Numbers

As we learned earlier, a lot of what we see in visions and dreams is symbolic in nature. In this chapter, you will find a list of common symbols, colors, numbers, and smells. Many symbols are subjective and can mean different things to different people. Often the same symbol will have a positive and a negative meaning. So the meaning must be deciphered in conjunction with the rest of the vision or dream.

Listed below are some common symbols and the most commonly accepted understanding of those symbols. Where feasible, I have included scripture references for those that are used as symbols in the Bible. Be aware that colors and symbols can have different meanings in different cultures. In my lists below, I have only included the meanings as generally understood in western culture. For example in western culture, red symbolizes passion, danger or stop-don't go ahead. In Chinese culture, red is a symbol of good luck and is often used at weddings as a symbol of happiness and prosperity for the new couple.

The understanding and meaning of these symbols has been gained through many years of deciphering my own visions and time that I have spent in research. I have read many other authors' works and listened to teaching on the prophetic by various speakers. Unfortunately, the origin of much that I have discovered has been forgotten. I have no wish to claim originality for all of these meanings. That would be unfair of me and untrue. I have listed some of the books that refer to these things, as I used those books to double-check the meanings.

You also need to learn how God speaks to you and to build your own list of symbols. To that end, we have provided pages at the end of this chapter for your own list.

Common Symbols
In visions and dreams

ANIMALS - Animals have different meanings, depending on the animal. For example:
Dove = symbol of Holy Spirit
Dogs = loyalty, friendship
Wolves = under attack
Ant = industrious.

ARMOR - Preparation for battle, defense against attack, protection while fighting (*Eph. 5:11-17*)
Armor too big = trying to fill someone else's role (*1Sam. 17:38-39*).

ARROWS - Wounds, words spoken against, witchcraft curses, striking at an enemy (*2 Kings 13:18*).

BABY - Innocence, new beginnings, inner nature, vulnerability, purity, naivety, immaturity.

BOOKS - Depending on type of book: wisdom, understanding, knowledge, revelation or frivolity and fantasy; judgement (*Rev. 20:12*); increase of knowledge (*Eccles. 12:12; 2 Tim. 3:7*).

BREAD - Revelation from God (*Deut. 8:3; Matt. 4*), provision of daily needs (*Luke 11:3*), self-effort (*Gen. 3:19*).

BROOM - Cleaning house, coming destruction (*Is. 14:23*).

CAR - Control issues (are you driving or a passenger?) Vehicle sometimes refers to your life, ministry, or business.

CAVES/HOLES & PITS -
Training place (*1 Sam. 22:1-3*), snare, false protection (*Jude 6:2*), prison (*Gen. 37:22*).

CHARIOT - Heavenly transport (*2 Kings 2:11*), heavenly warfare (*2 Kings 6:17*).

CLOCK - Time passing: be alert, watchful.

CLOTHING - Casual (comfortable), formal (sophisticated or stiff and starchy); can signify something about a person.

CROWDS - Peer pressure, public opinion, fear of man, status quo.

DAGGER - In hands of someone else = possible attack.
In your hands = defense or attack.
False word (not a sword).

DEATH - Not usually physical death: death to flesh,
insecurity, fear, evil intentions of enemy.

DONKEY - Humility, servant-hood, burden carrier, menial
work, overburdened.

DOORS/WINDOWS & PORTALS -
Entrance to or from spiritual realms (*Rev. 4:1;
Mal. 3:10*), new openings or ventures.

DRAGON - Demonic principalities or powers,
Satan (*Is. 27:1; Rev. 12:3-4; 7-9*).

EAGLES - Prophetic ability to see, mounting up (*Is. 40*),
renewed strength (*Ps. 103:5*).

EARTHQUAKE -
Shaking everything that can be shaken
(*Heb. 12:27*).

FATHER GOD -
(*Matt. 6:26*), security, provision (*Luke 11:11-12*).

FIELDS - Work, harvest (*John 4:35*), industry.

FIRE - Purifying, trials (*1 Peter 4:12*), cleansing (*Is.4:4*),
purging (*Mal. 3:2-3*), you'll get burned, attack for
an individual or group's destruction (*Dan. 3*).

FLYING - Overcoming, ascending, new areas opening to you, renewing strength (*Is. 40:31*), being transported.

FRUIT - Manifestations of the Holy Spirit (*Gal. 5:22*), fruit of individual or corporate lives.
If ripe = good fruit, ready to be harvested.
If spoiled = bad fruit, defiled.

GOLD - Glory of God, provision, wisdom, faith, false Gods (*Ex. 32:1-6*).

HOOKS - Links holding someone to the past.

HORSE - Strength, power, physical energy, arrogance.
Wild horse = freedom, lack of responsibility.
Tame horse = harnessed strength.
Dark horse = occult forces.
White horse = purity.

HOSPITAL - Healing, physical or mental health, fear of losing control.

HOUSE - Your personal life, family, dwelling place (*John 14:2*), home life, personality.
Attic = intellect
Basement = hidden beliefs, things hidden.
Bedroom = intimacy, privacy.
Bathroom = need for cleansing.

KEYS - Revelation (*Matt. 16:19*), new possessing.

MANTLE - Gifting or calling from God (*1Kings 19:19*), symbol of power (*2 Kings 2:8*), covering of God.

MEADOW - A place of rest (*Ps. 23*).

MIRROR - Self-focus, absorption, narcissism, seeing in a glass dimly (*1 Cor. 13:12*).

MONEY - Provision, abundance, lack of provision, lack of abundance, desire for security, power (*Matt. 6:21*).

MOTHER - Nurturing, love (*Prov. 4:3*).

OIL - Holy Spirit (*1 Sam. 16:13*), light (*Ex. 35:28*), anointing (*Ex. 29:7*), healing (*James 5:14*).

OVERCOAT -Covering, false mantle.

PEOPLE - Can relate to an area of your life, or prophetically, to someone else; feminine or masculine traits in a life.

PREGNANCY-
Conception, pregnant with vision, birth of something new or new phase in ministry (*Is. 43:19; 66:9*).

RIVER - River of life, river from the throne (*Rev. 22:1*), Ezekiel's river (*Ez. 47*), washing, healing, cleansing.

SCROLLS - Revelation, fresh direction, commissioning.

SEED - The word of God (*Matt. 13*), something planted or about to be, potential, descendants.
Good seed = children of Kingdom.
Tares = children of wicked one (*Matt. 13:38*).

SHOES OR FEET -
Gospel (*Is. 52:7*), taking ground, new ministry that you'll develop and grow in.
Shoes too big = trying to fill someone else's shoes.
Things under feet = dominion (*Ps. 8:6*).

SNAKES - Demonic powers, wisdom (*Matt. 10:16*).

SWORD - Word of God (*Eph. 6:14*), warrior, commissioning.

SUITCASE/BACKPACK-
Burdens, baggage

TENT - Impermanence, transitory, dwelling place
(*Is. 54:2*), speaks of the ability to move quickly or lack of being tied down by possessions; speaks of ability to expand easily (*Is. 54:2*).

TREES - Stability, planting (*Ps. 1:3*), nations, healing for nations (*Rev. 22:2*).
Fruit trees = fruit of a life or generation or civilization.

THRONE - Rule, authority (*1 Sam. 2:8*), justice & judgment (*Ps. 9:6; 89:14*).

TORNADO/WHIRLWIND-
Confusion (*2 Thess. 2:2*), scattering (*Jer. 49:32*), clearing unstable things away, shaking all that can be shaken (*Heb. 12:27*), the Lord moving (*Zech. 9:14*), heavenly transportation (*2 Kings 2:11*).

UMBRELLA -
Covering that is incomplete or only partially effective, false sense of protection.

VESSELS -   Mankind (*2 Cor. 4:7*), prayer (*Rev. 5:8*).

WINE -   Holy Spirit (*Eph. 5:18*), joy (*Ps. 4:7; 104:15*), laughter (*Eccles. 10:19*), offering (*Num. 15:10*), astonishment (*Ps. 60:3*), wickedness, violence (*Prov. 4:17*).

Colors

AMBER -   The glory of God, the brightness of His presence (*Ez. 1:4*).

BLACK -   Negative aspects of human life: death, disease, famine, sorrow, evil (*Job 30:30; Lam. 4:8*); lacking sense (*Prov. 7:9*), judgement, weighed in judgement (*Rev. 6:5*).

BLUE -   Heavenly things (*Ex. 24:9-11; Ez. 1:26*), commandments of God (*Num. 15:38-40*), holy service (*Ex. 28:31*), the bread of His presence (*Num. 4:5-7*), calm, confidence, power, conservatism.

BRONZE/COPPER -
Vessels, offerings (*Ex. 25:3*), refining, pillars of strength (*1 Kings 7:14-22*), lacking love (*1 Cor. 13:1*), strength in standing (*Rev. 1:15*).

BROWN/WOOD -
Human nature, the corruptible (*Ex. 26:15*), made acceptable covered by gold (*Ex. 26:29; 30:1-3*), rulership of Christ (*Is. 11:1*).

CRIMSON/SCARLETT-

Sin (*Jer. 23:5*), atonement, sacrifice (*Heb. 9:22; 1 John 1:7; Rev. 1:5*), cleansing and purification (*Lev. 14:4; Heb. 9:19-20*), color of the beast (*Rev. 17:3-6*).

GOLD -

That which is holy to God (*Ex. 28:36*), ark, mercy (*Ex. 25:10-11; 17-18*), wisdom (*Prov. 8:10; 16:16; 22:1*), faith (*1 Peter 1:7; Rev. 3:18*), greed, lust for riches.

GREY -

Respect, age (*Lev. 19:32; Prov. 20:29*), wisdom, experience (*Job 15:10*), sorrow or mourning (*2 Sam. 13:19; Esther 4:3*).

GREEN -

Flourishing, life, provision (*Gen. 1:30*), nations (*Ex. 17:24; Ez. 20:47*), fruitfulness (*Ps. 92:14*), rest (*Ps. 23:2-3*), envy or jealousy, renewal, environment, rest.

PURPLE -

Royalty, status (*Esther 8:15; Acts 16:14; Mark 15:17, 20; John 19:2*), riches (*Luke 16:19*), corruption (*Rev. 17:4; 18:6*).

RED -

Life (*Gen. 9:4-5; Deut. 12:23*), sin (*Is. 1:18*), judgement and warfare (*Nahum 2:3; Is. 62:1-6; Zech. 1:8; Rev 6:1; 9:7*), power, fame, danger.

VERMILLION/ORANGE -

Rich and ornate, extravagant, fire, lusts of human nature (*Jer. 22:13-14; Ez. 23*), false covering (*Matt. 23:27; Acts 23:2*), vibrancy, energy, warmth.

WHITE - Dazzling, clear, bright, like snow (*Mark 9:3; Rev. 7:14*), bride, the righteous (*Ps. 51:7; Dan. 7:9; Rev. 19:7-8*), purity, refining (*Ps. 51:7; Rev. 2:17*), overcoming (*Rev. 6:2; 19:11, 14*).

SILVER - Truth, understanding, fear of the Lord, knowledge of God (*Prov. 2:1-5; Ps. 12:6*), healing.

YELLOW - Joy, happiness, intellect, energy, false gold, false wisdom, leprous (*Lev. 13:30, 32, 36*), cowardice.

Numbers

1 - God, beginning, source, first, unity.

2 - Agreement, number of witnesses (in the mouth of two or more witnesses), friendship, double, multiplication.

3 - Godhead, trinity, divine completeness, perfect testimony.

4 - Creative works, the earth: four winds, four seasons, four corners of the earth.

5 - Grace, atonement, life, the cross, five-fold ministry.

6 - Number of man.

7 - Perfection, completeness, finished.

8 - New beginnings, put on new man, resurrection.

9 - Manifestation of the Spirit, harvest, ministry, fullness, fruitfulness, number of birthing (baby born in 9 months).

10 - Judgment, number of law, order, government, restoration, trial, testing, wilderness, tithe.

11 - Mercy.

12 - Divine government, apostolic fullness.

13 - Rebellion/backsliding, apostasy, revolution.

14 - Double anointing, double blessing, established

15 - Grace, spiritual order.

16 - Established, new beginning.

30 - Consecration, maturity for ministry, beginning ministry, call.

40 - Testing, ending in victory or defeat, wilderness ends.

50 - Jubilee, number of Pentecost, liberty, freedom.

666 - Antichrist, Satan, the beast.

Smells

ALCOHOL - A spirit of addiction, a need for deliverance.

ANTS - Industry, good works, new trails.

BREAD - Fresh word from God, revelation, provision.

BUBBLE GUM - Childlikeness.

BURNING - Good= fire of God; Bad= enemy, deception.

CIGARETTE SMOKE - Deliverance from addiction.

COFFEE - Awakening or time to wake up.

EGGS - Fresh = life
Rotten = decay

EUCALYPTUS/TEA-TREE - Healing.

FLOWERS - Heavenly realms.
Lily of the Valley, Rose of Sharon = Jesus

HONEY - Fresh revelation, presence of Jesus.

INCENSE - Sweet smelling = prayer.
Harsh smelling = prayers against.

LEATHER - New wineskins.

LEMONS - Refreshing.

OIL - Fresh oil = anointing, Holy Spirit.
Rancid oil = false anointing.

PERFUME - Jesus, Holy Spirit.
Stale perfume = religious spirit.

RAIN - Refreshing, blessings coming, washing clean.

ROSES - Jesus, lover of our soul; Jesus' bride.

SOAP - Cleansing.

VANILLA - Freshness, purity of word and revelation.

WINE - Holy Spirit.

For Further Study

Dreams & Visions - Jane Hamon
Seers Handbook - Sharnael Wolverton
The Prophets Dictionary - Dr. Paula Price
The Seer - James Goll
Dream Language - James Goll

There are also many sites on the internet with information regarding symbols, colors, numbers, and even smells.

Your Dictionary of Symbols

Use these pages to build your own dictionary of prophetic symbols.

Your Dictionary of Symbols

About the Author

*L*yn, along with her husband Rob, lead XP Ministries in New Zealand and are also itinerant ministers worldwide. Lyn has pastored alongside her husband in New Zealand in a variety of situations for over 30 years. They are both widely respected as prophetic ministers within New Zealand and internationally.

Lyn carries a catalytic, revelatory anointing that brings breakthroughs and shifts to individual lives and Churches as she ministers. Her teaching and ministry carries a very strong prophetic edge, calling and enabling people to step into their destiny as the glorious sons and daughters of God. Her heart is to see the Church walk in the fullness of all God has for them; releasing the Kingdom of Heaven into Earth and for them to have fun doing it.

Her prophetic gifting is expressed through her teaching (spoken and written), art, dance, story, and poetry. Lyn has written several books, covering a variety of subject matter, including poetry, a book on dance entitled *Free to Dance*, and two books of prophetic allegories called *Whispers from Heaven 1 & 2*. She has also produced teaching CD's on a variety of subjects. To find out more about any of these resources, contact Extreme Prophetic NZ, at the addresses below or go to the Extreme Prophetic webstore at www.extremeprophetic.com.

Contact Information

Please, do feel free to contact me and share some of your experiences and revelations. I would love to hear from you. I can be contacted at the addresses below.

Website – xpnewzealand.com
Email – lpacker@xpministries.com
Facebook Page – @creativepropheticcommunicator

CPSIA information can be obtained
at www.ICGtesting.com
Printed in the USA
BVHW041628281221
625051BV00010B/1219

9 781936 101290